THE
EXTRA-MILE
MANAGER

BEHAVIORAL ROI: ATTAINING IT ... SUSTAINING IT

JOSEPH COX

authorHOUSE®

AuthorHouse™
1663 Liberty Drive
Bloomington, IN 47403
www.authorhouse.com
Phone: 833-262-8899

Published by AuthorHouse 09/06/2023

ISBN: 979-8-8230-0956-0 (sc)
ISBN: 979-8-8230-0954-6 (hc)
ISBN: 979-8-8230-0955-3 (e)

Library of Congress Control Number: 2023910274

Print information available on the last page.

CONTENTS

ABOUT THE READER

If you are a manager, you may wonder how your behavior toward your staff affects their productivity and your department's contribution to profit. If so, this book is for you. The author had many loathsome jobs. Apathetic managers aggravated poor work conditions. He was aggrieved enough to spend most of his adult life deciphering the real-world (bottom-line) metrics from bosses' behaviors toward those under their care. The absence of accountability for ill-treatment of staff, with consequent poor productivity, has been a universal norm. Still, many managers act in their people's best interests. What measurable difference does that make?

Metrics on intangible inputs are hard to come by, which is why this book spans almost four decades. There are many behavioral needles in the corporate haystack. To isolate the ones that raise productivity and profit, the author measured a wide range of behavioral inputs for their impact. Audited financial statements over the span of research projects are empirical evidence of impact. Correlation studies are summarized for readers. Measurable behavioral change is slow, so time is squeezed. But positive signs emerged within the first year of introducing behavioral metrics that raise accountability. The un-engagement mystery was solved in the process. It's good old-fashioned *caring* behavior that turns red ink black. Apathetic managers exude red ink. It will shock you to know how much. It comes down to where you—and all managers–are on the apathy-empathy continuum. Managers are not stuck. Positive behavioral change is doable.

When you get to the bottom line, and the last chapter, you'll have a handle on the negative intangible inputs that plague enterprises. You will have a leg up on everyone who didn't digest this book. You'll know what your staff needs from you, so you can up your game. They will love you for providing it. And your firm? It will credit you for opening the spigot to a whole new source of profit. Shouldn't managers have a behavioral algorithm to max out results? It's here. As you apply it, you'll be going the extra mile for your people. They will reciprocate. Your numbers will validate your impact in exact dollars, proof of your effectiveness.

INTRODUCTION

ABOUT THE AUTHOR AND THE BOOK

If you are reading this introduction to decide whether to acquire this book, you may want to know how the saga chronicled here began. That's me at our home in Boggy Creek, Florida, near today's Disney World.

At the time of this picture, my parents were picking oranges to make ends meet. Neither went to high school but went to work after the eighth grade. Yet from this humble beginning, under their parenting, in a culture of poverty, I found a life purpose in my late teens. Puberty had been rocky. I had imagined myself in various lines of work, but nothing could maintain my interest for more than a few days. I didn't know why, but I had to know. Finally, the day came, when exasperated, I sank to my knees and groaned, "Oh God, what's the answer?" It wasn't a prayer. Just an exclamation. But I got an answer.

I suddenly knew that I had to communicate a message. I did not know what it was or who the audience would be. But I knew I would speak and write it. Who knows how we can just know something? But it's so strong that we can't deny it. It would be denying who we are. I became a different person that day. I had to find out what I stood for and who most needed to hear it. It never left my head but it took twenty-one years to get a grip on it. I wasn't passionate about anything in particular. Purpose would slowly become a conscious perception.

In the intervening period, I would earn a B.S. Degree. I would get married and move to South Africa. I would be in an MBA program there (the M is a misnomer in at least one skill). I was divorced after 17 years. The impact on us and our three children would be lengthy and trying. I'd be a club rugby forward for 11 years, a high school physics teacher and head high school rugby coach for six years. I would spend ten years in management positions and start two businesses—building houses and farming.

After all this, and at this point in my life, the first chapter of *The Extra-Mile Manager* begins. The book spans almost four decades. Today, it all makes total sense. The clarity about purpose is exhilarating. I'm fulfilling it—still. But not alone. If purpose is noble, it is never selfish. And if it's unselfish, others help us attain it.

Beyond my personal experiences, this book is about you and for you, my readers. If you are in management, it's about those who work for you. It's also for the firms we work for and their shareholders. The epitome of conclusions that I wish every reader to make is this: *What we put into our people is what we get out of them. In very large measure, they determine how well our enterprises will succeed.* We prove that here empirically, with statistics that drive the point home.

Purpose gets much clearer if we marry someone with a skill-set we don't have—one that compliments ours. Complimentary skills enrich efforts and outputs. Work is more on-purpose. That's a big motivator. We accomplish more at better quality. More people benefit from our work.

Joseph Cox   Regina Rodriguez

But it's also about passion—the one big, noble quest that pulls out our best. My life partner is Regina Rodriguez, a medical doctor certified in occupational health, with experience in transnational firms in Latin America and offshore. This prepared her, as we conducted three multiyear studies linking work needs' satisfaction metrics with firms' productivity and profit. Her heart is in this work as well as mine. It's been a fruitful 20 years.

We collect voluminous data. We correlate input stats with output stats, find anomalies that should correlate but don't, and then investigate *why not* through research partner firms. Every anomaly is highlighted and followed up. Underlying causes are identified and resolved. We know when they are— because productivity and profit rise.

Twenty-seven years of field studies (including a 17-year solo study) all yielded the same outputs when we identified the behavioral inputs that mattered. My message became *caring about our people*— in particular about their work needs. My audience became *management*. Our mission is to improve the quality of relevant care. As we drilled into that, we found that the intensity and frequency of care are critical. If people aren't feeling it, we aren't enriching their employee experience. The benefit to firms from institutionalizing care, as set out here, is doubling net profit (thereabouts) within three years.

This is my tenth book. After various R&D milestones, I chronicled processes and statistics, and tools developed enroute. Spanish readers might check out *Lo Que No Aprendi en mi MBA* (2007). Translated: *What I Didn't Learn in My MBA*. For English readers, check out *Nail It Today with Both Hands* (2013) on Amazon. *The Extra-Mile Manager* is my third book since Regina joined me. She vetted every line of every manuscript and brought clarity, succinctness, and pragmatism to complex intangibles. Much credit due. The Spanish edition is a thank-you (and reinforcement) for Latin American partners who offered their firms as R&D laboratories to entrench work-needs equity.

The book is very compact, and it is not a quick read. It is written to be digested and applied. If not, truth is wasted. Truth changes people and companies. When we apply it, forecasted results materialize. Over the next three years, readers can see miracles from metrics by granting peoples' legitimate work needs. We developed the tools to assist you.

Truth is obfuscated by a management misconception concerning employees: "We know what's best for you."

Excuse me, but we don't. We are not in their chairs or at their workbenches. We do not do their type of work. We do not interact with their colleagues nor with many of their supervisors. We do not feel expendable. We do not get their salaries and they lack many of our benefits. We do not read their minds. Only they know what they want. But we haven't asked them because we already know.

Jacob Harold, cofounder of Candid, articulates it well:

> Have a feedback loop that is qualitative, that is human. The best way to do that is to ask the people who you're trying to serve if what you're doing is helping and to have your ears open to signals that something's back-firing.

Unengaged and disengaged staff tell us that something's backfiring. Data tell us precisely what that is. We feed results back to managers, along with strategies to remove satisfaction impediments and trigger work motivators. Work becomes meaningful and more rewarding. Productivity rises.

The Extra-Mile Manager tackles the world's costliest business problem— unengaged and disengaged employees. Gallup, Inc. reported that in 2022, US engagement was 32 percent. It's more abysmal everywhere else. No firm has solved this statistical malady. We take the mystery out of the enigma. Applying proven strategies introduced here turns mediocre managers into high performers, who turn staff into high performers. Every manager's and member's best gifts should be in action. Shouldn't that be the norm?

The difference in productivity that comes from high motivation is astounding. It becomes a third source of profit. For CFOs, the Third Bucket of Profit equals profit from gross margin and expense control *combined*. CFOs and financial controllers must control all three buckets of profit. Annual reports should rank bucket 3 on a par with margins and expense control. Accordingly, auditors should investigate it and report on it. It is a high-ranking key performance indicator (KPI). In this book, we call it the productivity index (PI). We calculate that differently than the US Department of Labor—for motivational reasons.

The revelations in *The Extra-Mile Manager* are compelling. Despite the billions spent annually to change managers' behavior, inequity, un- engagement, staff turnover and toxic climates persist. The technology emerging from this research leaves no wiggle room for uncaring managers. We trace red ink directly to apathy for people's work needs. When managers deny the legitimate needs identified in this research, corrective action must follow. Hard facts on every manager's behavior enables tailored strategies. Where do we get our facts to work with? Exhaustive research and the people who work for us. Listening to them is transformational.

I hope my readers are ready for an interesting, enlightening, and paradigm-changing ride. That's what it has been, and still is, for us.

1

AFRICAN ORIGINS

One of the scariest things in the world, is that other people can make life-changing decisions for you.

—KARISHMA MAGVANI

I WAS STANDING IN THE OFFICE of Alec Rogoff, managing director (MD) of Beares Ltd., in Durban, South Africa. He had just asked me two questions that felt like they threatened my job:

> "How much did you spend on the leadership program for our managers?"

> "How much increased profit has been generated from the program?"

The second question was scarier than the first. I answered the first one on the spot: "Just shy of a million dollars."

He followed up: "We have 1,300 company vehicles—not enough. We could buy another fifty trucks with that million, and we need them. We're opening new stores."

It was late 1982. Five tonners for delivering furniture were about $20,000 each (the South African rand was roughly equivalent to the US dollar at that time). He gave me thirty days to report back on his second question and then ended the *meeting*.

Beares was the best company I ever worked for. It was a super employee experience with a great boss. My position was the group training manager for 7,500 employees, including a thousand managers. The program we bought (before I was hired) is still popular in the United States and abroad. I trained managers in it throughout Southern Africa. Participant evaluations were positive, but that didn't help my quandary. My job was on the line because I couldn't do what no one else could do either. Was it fair to fire me over that? Yet the MD was right. Why are we doing this if we can't prove it has a measurable return? I was certain that I only had a month left. I couldn't afford to waste it.

If your job is on the line, how could you document the financial impact of leadership training? If you take the journey with me to the end of this book, we'll reason that question through together. Shall we start by talking to the managers who participated in the leadership program? What did they do with it?

I started setting appointments, two per day, with furniture store managers within an hour's drive of Durban. Forty interviews over the next month ought to yield examples of use and possible outcomes, or reasons why it wasn't used. Managers had more than a year to apply the program.

Many leadership programs teach managers to adapt their styles to staff needs for direction and support. But performance issues multiply fast if managers have several staff members, each with different tasks and different levels of proficiency in each. Applying the right style on the spot required instant recall of training content from workshops conducted more than a year before. Application required real-time versatility in style. When the rubber met the road, the training didn't transfer to the job. Well before the last interview, outcomes were obvious—no utility so no ROI.

All forty managers defaulted to their normal styles. We pulled them off the job, trained them thoroughly—spent big bucks on it—but it didn't supplant their natural styles. We didn't test program content on the front line before rolling it out corporate-wide. A million dollars gone. But that's the way things were done back then. It's still common.

We'll learn about other training efforts lacking measurable correlation with profit as we advance together. Here's a clue about them: Nowhere do the companies or their managers ask staff what they want from management. Management decides how its managers will manage their staffs' performances. Just a thought: Before we develop a new product, shouldn't we find out what our customers and end users need and want?

My scheduled meeting with Mr. Rogoff was the day after my last interview. At least I had something to report, even with no ROI on the $1M. With little sleep and my nerves on edge, his secretary showed me in. I summarized my findings and waited for Mr. Rogoff's decision. Mercifully, the *other* Mr. Rogoff surfaced: "I knew you would find no link to profit. I knew it wasn't your call to buy it."

Then he laid out an unnerving challenge that would immerse me in a mission until this book: "Figure out how to make managers' training stick. Staff turnover is bleeding us dry. What is it they want from us that we're not giving them?"

An astute, crucial project to plunge into, with questions that defy answers, plus endless trial-and-error studies to nail causes and effects. I saw its elusiveness instantly. It would be a hard row to hoe, all-consuming. Entirely new ground. Oddly, that made it more motivating than foreboding.

I told Mr. Rogoff it was the kind of challenge that turned me on. I thanked him for the learning experience and the chance to work on something salient for Beares and firms everywhere.

I walked out fundamentally reoriented. Thinking about it while driving home, I guessed it would take seven years to correlate training in soft skills with profit. It took more than five times that. I'm enthused that readers will share the discovery process with me. Every chapter ahead is a milestone on the quest to answer Mr. Rogoff's poignant questions.

Over the next year and a half, I tackled them as assigned. I wouldn't know the success of the innovations I introduced at Beares for another five years. It took twelve years after that to measure the full impact on Beares' bottom line.

Let's now leapfrog to the 2020s. His questions are still being asked universally. The reader will be in the middle of this quest to answer them. Let's put our heads together.

2

EXTRINSIC SMORGASBORD

Waste of resources is a mortal sin at IKEA.

—INGVAR KAMPRAD,
IKEA FOUNDER

We'll RETURN TO THE BEARES story in a later chapter. Let's fast-forward to the workforce motivation issue as it's being grappled with in the 2020s. The hot intangible topic today is termed *engagement*. That's when people are so motivated that they give discretionary effort, not just the minimum for a paycheck.

Wasted resources concern every business. But one waste in every business isn't controlled, not even at IKEA. Two-thirds of people give a fraction of their capacity. Firms must hire extra people to do the work. That drives profits down by half, as we'll see. Managers' soft skills are falling short despite trainloads of revenues to inculcate them.

As the reader likely knows, serious study on motivation began 125 years ago with Frederick Taylor, the *'Father of Scientific Management'*. *Engagement* was not the word used back then, *motivation* was. It was clear that motivation counted. Taylor sought a scientific solution to offer business owners. Regrettably, his work made no measurable difference.

Was it science as we understand it today—that is, evidence-based cause and effect? That is our approach here.

With Taylor's work in mind, Mayo, Maslow, McGregor, Herzberg, and Drucker further postulated, in order, up through the year 2000. Most managers have been exposed to at least one of these gurus' models. Regrettably, these scholars' works weren't effectively implemented, so they could not be traced to the bottom line. That may leave the reader wondering, as I have, where it all ends. Still, let's not give up here. Solutions are attained by perseverance. Shall we trek on with a question similar to the MD's 1982 mind-bender?

Why are two-thirds of US employees still unengaged or disengaged?

Would the reader agree it's a pressing need to find out what's been missing? With your responses (√) to these questions, let's try to clarify at least one thing overlooked:

	More	Less
1. If staff thinks their manager has no integrity and fails to guide and support them as needed, will they be more or less inclined to give discretionary effort.		
2. If staff thinks their manager has integrity and guides and supports them as needed, will they be more or less inclined to give discretionary effort?		
3. If staff believes their manager treats them fairly and they have a sense of belonging with colleagues, will they be more or less inclined to give discretionary effort?		
4. If staff is making use of their best skills in their job, will they be more or less inclined to give discretionary effort?		
5. If their manager provides development opportunities for them, will staff be more or less inclined to give discretionary effort?		

Answers may not be black or white. On some, we don't know for sure. But answers do suggest what *might* be missing. Is there a question you checked "less" to? Was it number 1? It's the only question where needs are not being met. Is that a possible indication that a correlation between work need satisfaction and discretionary effort (engagement) exists? Let's take that hypothesis a step further: *Staff gives more of what management wants when management gives more of what the staff needs and wants.* If that is so, who must initiate giving?

What would be the next key question? Take a minute. How about this one? Why are managers more concerned about their own needs than their staffs' needs? Take another minute. Because we are all just like managers. More out to get than give. Does this natural behavior serve us well at work, or elsewhere for that matter? Solutions must consider the human condition. It affects interpersonal relations. Self-interest may negate others' interests. Would that affect engagement, which is rooted in relationships? The reader probably, and correctly, surmised that the crucial relationships are:

- Between a staff member and his or her manager
- Between a staff member and his or her colleagues
- Between staff members' work talents and the content of their jobs and tasks

Suboptimal relationships negatively impact job performance. That's intuitive, right? With many people unengaged, surely management (we) noticed *something* was missing. And what did we think it was? Did we investigate and explain how things or perks improve relationships? How did they trigger discretionary effort? Check out these employee benefits (things) management added over the last hundred years to keep staff optimally functioning:

Equal employment opportunity	D-E-I policy and training
Paid holidays	Paid health insurance
Maternity leave for both parents	12 day's sick leave or more
Pension plans, 401K's	Profit sharing
Flex time	Work remotely
Tuition reimbursement	Shift differential pay
Protection from sexual harassment, abuse and wrongful termination	In-house skills training
Promote from within policy	Performance and annual bonuses
Cafeterias	Travel allowance

Most are optional, but a few are federally mandated. We've come a long way from the six-day, sixty-five-hour workweek in 1850. One would think that human resources ought to be flying through their tasks with aplomb, enthusiasm, and optimal use of time. The annual engagement survey numbers from Gallup Inc. refute that notion:

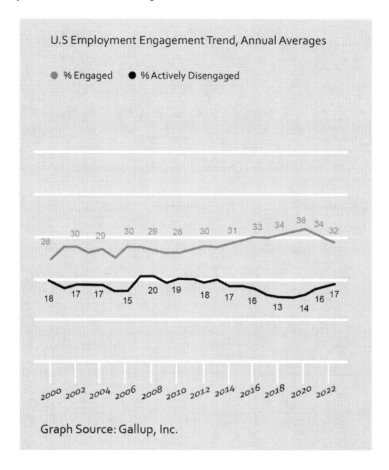

U.S Employment Engagement Trend, Annual Averages

● % Engaged   ● % Actively Disengaged

Graph Source: Gallup, Inc.

We have pretty much flatlined. To date, there is no engagement cure from things. Labor/management issues still simmer. Gallup's engagement needle did take a twenty-one-year baby step in the right direction. Yet, if the steps and the pace continue as shown, in 2122 we'll reach 86 percent engaged. Things don't appear to incentivize extra effort. Running out of things to try can't be far down the road. We laud every benefit that management has granted their people. It was generous. Our purpose here is defining the *kind* of benefits that motivate people and generate ROI.

Beyond what consulting firms offer to cure un-engagement, organizations globally try their own solutions. In the United States, we hire over 200,000 new MBA graduates annually. (Surely grad school professors have nailed solutions.) Besides these masters, we have doctors - thousands of PhDs running organizational development (OD) departments.

> *Factoid:* Mastery, as in master of business administration, omits actual motivational mastery.

Getting down to brass tacks, with the brainpower of the C-suite, coupled with what behavioral scientists advocate, we reduced active disengagement (hostility) by 1 point out of 100 over twenty-two years. That statistic leaves us shocked, given the cost and effort invested. To be fair to everyone working on this, intangibles, like motivation, are very slippery to measure; I pulled out a lot of hair. Until we can do that, we won't be able to precisely define gaps, set standards, or assign accountability. Every manager who is a few bricks short on relationships, as we all are, gets a pass. Higher revenues for payroll will continue to erode profits.

The Extra-Mile Manager grew out of a series of studies, sparked at Beares and different in its kind. The first foot I put forward, but not the last, is what people need and want (courtesy, Mr. Rogoff). Following the interventions in 1983 under apartheid in South Africa, I continued with multiyear studies in Central America and the Caribbean. The latest, a three-year research project, concluded in Mexico in October 2021. Interspersed were a range of micro-studies with large US firms.

Conditions in the laboratory firms were not ideal, even troubling. That was advantageous in retrospect. After South Africa, I knew I needed stringent, immersive effort and perseverance to isolate the key variables affecting engagement. Where the rubber meets the road needed scrutiny on every initiative. The more adverse the conditions, the more to be learned.

We unveil findings as they emerged. Readers can judge their prudence, virtue, and fruit. We now know that work needs are big eye-openers. They are prominent, specific, and universally common. We list them and share how we compiled them. To date, management hasn't understood their role in engagement: They govern management/staff relations. Can readers almost hear workforces saying, "If you don't care about our work needs, we don't care about what you need"?

> *Factoid: People don't care how much you know until they know how much you care.*
>
> *(Theodore Roosevelt)*

The engagement solution is in the human psyche, not in tangible benefits. As nice as they are, the latter doesn't fire up enthusiasm for the job itself. That's a different bucket of motivators we'll learn to call *intrinsic*. Shall we take a deep dive into the corporate intangible universe?

3

SPOTLIGHT ON INTANGIBLES

*There are intangible realities which float
near us, formless and without words; realities
which no one has thought out, and which
are excluded for lack of interpreters.*

—NATALIE CLIFFORD BARNEY

As READERS LIKELY HAVE EXPERIENCED, intangibles are easy-to-ignore phenomena; they don't jump out at us. Our default mode is to leave them alone. Yet, they don't leave us alone. To salvage wasted payroll dollars, we must get a handle on the complex, untethered world of intangibles.

What is the real problem with them? Readers could list a range of problems. Does your list overlap with mine?

- There are myriad behavioral inputs to corporate productivity.
- They are in constant motion.
- Gray areas abound.
- Emotions cloud issues and facts.
- They affect metrics, but we don't know which intangibles generate which metrics.

- When we explore, behavioral rabbit trails beckon, then disappoint—one after another.
- Isolating behavioral causes is almost as elusive as reading minds.

These explain why curious thinkers peek inside and then hustle back to tangible reality. An analogy is apropos:

> Let the reader imagine being a marriage counselor. You want to know what percentage of each of the wife's and husband's behaviors contributed to their spouse's decision to seek, or agree to, a divorce. Knowing that, you could salvage more marriages by reducing or increasing certain partner behaviors. Spouses must like each other's input for the relationship to survive.

> The clue hanging out there is what each party wanted. Whatever it was, as with unengaged associates, the spouses weren't getting it. The only one who could give it was the other spouse, but it wasn't forthcoming. Couples are motivated to get engaged and motivated to disengage. With the current divorce rate near the un-engagement rate in the United States, managers and marriage counselors have similar results and challenges. Terminations and resignations are the broken marriages of the corporate world. They may also be sad and costly.

The Roman Emperor Marcus Aurelius, wrote in *Meditations*, "The secret of all victory is the organization of the non-obvious."

Subjectivity is the norm in the intangible world. Ambiguity thrives on it, leaving all of us puzzled about what to do. Sensory, emotional, and bias factors can be costly, like disengagement. Until we learn how to identify them, dislodge them (behaviors resist change), or negate their impacts, extra profit from intangible sources will elude us. The MD's questions still beg for answers.

Our task is identifying and measuring the relevant behaviors in the mix of intangibles. If readers can resolve this enigma in their workplaces, the metrics generated help to increase behaviors (motivations) that serve your interests and decrease those that don't. Satisfaction of work needs enhances relationships and is crucial in engaging staff. To get our minds around this task, it's similar to customer service.

Good customer service means qualitatively satisfying all customer needs as they surface. Customer needs may be repetitive, cyclic, or random. New needs can pop up anytime. Satisfying them keeps the customer engaged with us. It's a reciprocal give-and-take relationship. When customers are pleased with what we give them, they respond favorably. It can become a durable, win-win relationship, based on serving. That's important to sustain current profits, and is why meeting staff's needs enhances our bottom lines. Let's define the inputs on work needs more precisely.

Ambiguity morphs into facts when we introduce targeted stimuli that elicit predictable responses. (We address reciprocity in chapter 8.) Our studies showed that high intensity and high frequency of managers' behaviors to satisfy their staffs' work needs increase productivity *over time*. We measure it with the productivity index (chapter 9). When managers are the first to give, they initiate the receiving process, which stimulates discretionary effort from staff.

Readers likely assume that a staff's work needs are also cyclic, repetitive, or random. One can pop up out of the blue, which makes the frequency and strength of actions equally critical for staff's needs satisfaction. The survey (covered later) is the assessment instrument I developed to capture and organize the nonobvious. It measures the frequency and intensity of work needs to three sigmas of variance each. A three-sigma variance from the norm (satisfied need) puts a staff member into a negative mindset. The need is intense and frequent (a double whammy). The manager is unaware, doesn't care, or both. The relationship sours, and engagement, if it was there, devolves into un-engagement or disengagement. Productivity measurably declines.

Assessment works in tandem with development. To improve the quality of actions to meet staff work needs, we developed a virtual university. The competencies—soft skills and professional skills—target work needs. As they are inculcated and mastered, soft-skill metrics become as hard as any tangible factor that impacts the bottom line.

All parties in the supply chain for work need satisfiers have less capacity to meet customer needs if their own needs aren't being met. It happens in front of us, but we don't see it. Yet if it were a customer's need, we would hop on it right now. We forfeit revenue if we don't.

> *Factoid: We won't fall short on customer needs, just on the staff responsible for meeting those needs.*

Shouldn't managers show their staff the same care they want customers to receive, for the same reason—it's profitable? Managers' actions generate red or black ink due to correlations with falling or rising productivity from staff. Few behaviors used with staff are neutral.

As readers can appreciate, management is about where we are going and what our staff needs along the way. Without strong, frequent, qualitative direction and support, discretionary effort won't materialize.

We'll periodically repeat the following to embed it:

> Every unsatisfied work need means money is going into payroll that should be going to profit. Or future profit is being forfeited by defaulting on customer needs.

Under what fiduciary rationale can management decline to institutionalize needs-equity? Shareholders might ask that question at board or shareholder meetings.

This era since COVID-19 is being called the "Great Resignation," and more recently the "Great Attrition." Historically, it will be seen as an *event*. It follows an epochal paradigm we call *"The Great Gap."* It's the void between what workers want and what is. People want fulfilling jobs. That takes satisfaction from intrinsic motivators. What exists is management's historic inability to close that gap. Past efforts at providing new benefits left The Great Gap intact. Those who were able launched out on their own, driven by hungry psyches and avoidance of management's apathy for their work needs if they returned.

Since 2000, Gallup, Inc. has labeled the intrinsic gap as "un-engagement." People who love their jobs don't tender resignations. For the disheartened, COVID-19 was the chance to seek intrinsic satisfaction by working remotely or by plying their talents in self-employment. Millions of people sacrificed fifteen extrinsic benefits, that management had extended in the last 100 years, to be autonomous, creative, challenged. Will we get them back and keep them with another extrinsic—signing bonuses? Why not promise inspiration by giving them the chance to thrive and flourish by using their best skills, by being a partner in profit? Why not then go the extra mile and deliver it?

In chapter 6, we list the work needs that, when satisfied, correlate highly with productivity. In chapter 7, we contrast two very different ways organizations address low engagement.

My Employee Experience

At age eleven, I got a job with a local newspaper. Monday through Saturday, I delivered a hundred papers by bicycle. But the Sunday edition was three to four times thicker than the daily. A hundred papers wouldn't fit into the canvas bags hanging from my handlebars, so my supervisor assisted with her car.

She picked me up at 4:00 Sunday morning. Before 6:00, we had to deliver the papers. To fit into the *News Journal* boxes at the curb, the papers had to be folded. Not a problem for the weekday editions. But folding the Sunday edition was nearly impossible for me. My supervisor pulled up to her house with me in the passenger seat and a hundred papers in the back seat. She told me to fold them all and put rubber bands around them; then she disappeared into her house. I reached over to the backseat and grabbed a paper. The grief started.

My hands were too small and weak to fold them enough to get rubber bands around them. One rubber band after another broke, stinging my fingers, stiff from the unusually cold weather in Florida. I knew a big problem with my supervisor was looming. She returned around 5:00 a.m. to find three folded, banded papers. She screamed about how "lazy and irresponsible" I was. She grabbed a paper, folded it, and put a rubber band on it—in five seconds. "What's so hard about that?" she asked. I had to tell Dad and Mom, who helped me get the job, that I got fired.

Two questions about work needs: Can the person do the job as offered? What does the person need to do the job? I discovered at home that I could fold and band a Sunday paper using a larger rubber band. I might have folded about thirty and maybe thirty more as we drove the route. I might have kept the job. I held back the tears until 6:00 a.m. They poured down when I got out of her car.

As readers work through to the end of *The Extra-Mile Manager*, we'll explore biology, psychology, social anthropology, statistics, and the power of purpose. Let's tackle biology first in a short but potent chapter on primal behaviors.

4

PROSOCIAL PRIMATES

*Everything is improved by the judicious
application of primates.*

— CHRIS ROBERSON

SOME OF THE BEHAVIORS AFFECTING relationships between managers and staff stem from DNA. We are predisposed to want and expect what we consider to be fair behavior from others, especially those with the power to grant or deny our needs. At a minimum, we expect equal treatment with others in our group. We also really appreciate selfless behavior from others—altruism—when someone does something for us but expects nothing in return. When we receive it, we are inclined to return the favor. But if we are treated unfairly, are slighted, or are denied something we feel is a right or simply a normal need, we reciprocate in kind—with opposition and disengagement. We may aggregate resistance as a disgruntled group, clandestinely or openly. We exhibit disrespect, even spite, for management if their offenses are egregious enough. Failing to control these phenomena in the workplace comes with a punishing price tag.

Where did humans get these behaviors? You might be thinking, *discussing fairness, altruism, reciprocity, and spite sounds more like the topics for a labor relations conference, not something biological.* True, but the origins are genetic. These positive and negative traits are inside us all, without exception. They are as old as our species. They are what we are as homo sapiens, what we fight for or against, and what we do when needs and desires are denied. These behaviors manifest naturally at work, and they directly impact outcomes. Results ensuing from them are measurable on the balance sheet, as we meticulously examine throughout *The Extra-Mile Manager*.

Fairness and altruism are in our cousins as we shall see. Reciprocity is also there in a limited sense. So far, spite seems to be uniquely human, but we once thought that about altruism. We are the clothed hominids in the corporate zoo. And we have issues with zookeepers. They can make us enthusiastic or resentful. We will reciprocate either way, and if it's against real ogres, we will be spiteful. Red ink will flow.

There appears to be a universal sense of fairness in primates. We hear kids playing games when one suddenly sounds the alarm, "Hey that's not fair!" Why do we automatically appeal to a standard of fairness? Who set the standard for it? How did it become the yardstick to govern interpersonal relations? Our cousins have the same issue with unfairness. Capuchin monkeys throw a fit when one of their companions gets a better treat.

In experiments conducted by Emory and Georgia State Universities, thirteen Capuchin monkeys were the subjects in a fairness behavioral study. Pairs of monkeys were placed in adjacent cages so that each monkey could clearly see the other monkey. The pairs were trained to hand a small granite rock to an observer in exchange for a treat. Treats were of two types—a piece of cucumber or a grape. All monkeys regarded the grape as the superior of the two treats.

There was no issue if both monkeys handed over the stone and both received a piece of cucumber in return. But if one monkey received a grape and the other a piece of cucumber, the one that received the cucumber threw it back at the observer. *Envy* reared its ugly head. The video of the experiment, narrated by Dr. Frans de Waal of Emory, is amusing. All too human. Researchers conclude that recognizing an unfair situation and reacting strongly to it may be critical for maintaining relationships in cooperative societies, like those of capuchins and humans.

> "In a cooperative species, being able to distinguish when one is being treated in-equitably is very useful for determining whether or not to continue cooperating with a partner."

> "This work resonates with a lot of people, because I think all of us have had those experiences where something seems good enough until we found out that someone had a higher salary or a better start-up package." (Jeanna Bryner, quoting Sarah Brosnan. *Live Science,* November 12, 2007. www.emory.edu/ LIVING_LINKS/LL_2009/inequitypress1.html)

Equal opportunity, equal treatment laws stem from this same innate penchant for fairness as the *arch lord arbiter*. Whoever heard a lawyer argue that unfairness didn't matter? Have you ever been jealous of the teacher's pet? How about the boss's favorite if it isn't you? Who gets the plum projects to work on? Who gets the onerous ones? Who is paid more for doing the same work as everyone else?

These situations are common, and associates often have little option but to accept them. But the story isn't over. Unfairness is remembered. There is a lingering need to rectify inequity. Unfairness influences cooperation and work output. When there are multiple inequities, strong resentments form. We are instinctively less supportive of those who slight us. It comes from way back. It won't change. It is in our DNA. Management must play fair or reap red ink.

Altruism has a notch up on fairness because it comes with a price to someone who shows it. What if the observer in the Capuchin monkey experiment had only one grape and one piece of cucumber between the two monkeys? But if the observer took a grape from his own lunch to make the aggrieved monkey feel better, that would be an act of altruism. Many studies show that humans prefer romantic partners who are altruistic.

> "Emory conducted further behavioral experiments using chimps as subjects, to see if altruism is innate to other primates. In these simplified experiments, two chimps were housed in immediate proximity but separated by a transparent screen so they could see each other. A bin containing tokens of two different colors was available to one chimp only. One color token could be exchanged with an experimenter for a reward for both chimps. This choice was called the prosocial option—the altruistic one. The other color token could be exchanged for a reward only for the chimp with the tokens—the selfish option. The reward was a piece of banana wrapped in paper. The paper made a crackling noise when removed, letting chimps know that another was benefiting from their action." (https://www.livescience.com/15451-chimps-humanlike-altruism.html)

The study used seven adult female chimps placed into various pairs. The researchers found that all chimps showed a clear preference for the altruistic (prosocial) option. "For me, the most important finding is that like us, chimpanzees take into account the needs and wishes of others," researcher Victoria Horner, a comparative psychologist at Emory University, told *LiveScience.*

Dr. Frans de Waal adds, "the idea that chimps are indifferent to the welfare of others can now hopefully be put to rest."

> "The chimps were particularly altruistic toward partners who either patiently waited or gently reminded them that they were there by drawing attention to themselves. They were less likely to reward partners who exerted pressure by making a fuss, begging persistently or spitting water at them … It was far more productive

for partners to be calm and remind the choosers they were there from time to time." (https://www.livescience. com/15451-chimps-humanlike-altruism.html)

So, chimps are sensitive to whether or not an individual deserves a handout. Among chimps, as with humans, those who are annoyingly demanding get shunned. Horner adds more insight:

> "This is interesting because there has been a long-standing view that the chimpanzees only share food under pressure. Our results suggest the opposite—chimpanzees share when there is no to little pressure, but direct pressure or threats reduce sharing, possibly due to negative emotions. Our results are subtly different. When you provide assistance, it's really a test between doing something or nothing. In our study, the chimps really have three choices—they can do nothing, they can be prosocial, or they can be selfish."

Researchers say these findings, and those from other studies, demonstrate that many primate species have similar tendencies and that altruism has deeper genetic origins than previously thought* (http://www.livescience. com/15451-chimps-humanlike-altruism.html).

Another study of note involves chimps interacting with humans who have needs. If they were to show prosocial behavior to humans, then the behavior is generalized, therefore, firmly embedded in their psyches, not just a clan cultural phenomenon in the wild. Researchers studied thirty-six chimps born in the wild but living at Ngamba Island Chimp Sanctuary in Uganda:

> "Each chimp was put in a position to watch a complete stranger unsuccessfully try to reach a wooden stick that was within reach of the chimp. The human had

---

* Horner and de Waal also detailed their findings online on August 8, 2010, in the *Proceedings of the National Academy of Sciences.*

attempted to reach for the stick beforehand, indicating it was valuable. Researchers observed that the chimps often handed the stick over, even if they had to climb eight feet out of their way to get the stick, and whether or not any reward was given. Researchers obtained similar results with 36 human infants at just 18 months old."

"Chimps will help strangers at personal cost to themselves without any personal gain, a level of selfless behavior thought until now to be unique to humans. Scientists assume altruism evolved to help those willing and able of returning the favor - to help either one's kin or oneself. Humans occasionally help strangers with no apparent benefit to themselves, and often at great cost." (https://www.livescience.com/4515-selfless-chimps-shed-light-evolution-altruism.html)

Felix Warneken, of the Max Planck Institute for Evolutionary Anthropology, sums it up:

"There is a biological predisposition to altruistic tendencies that we share with our common ancestor, and culture cultivates rather than implants the roots of altruism in the human psyche from primordial forms to more mature ones." (http://www.livescience.com/4515-selfless-chimps-shed-light-evolution-altruism.html)

Several studies on the temporoparietal junction of the brain (TPJ) show a biological source of altruistic behavior. One study found a strong connection between the size of a subject's TPJ and his or her willingness to act selflessly. The larger the TPJ, the more likely subjects were to behave altruistically. One study involving thirty "normal" healthy adults played a series of games in which they could increase or decrease their partners' monetary reward. While subjects participated, observing and making decisions at specific points, their TPJs were monitored by functional MRIs measuring blood oxygen levels where nerve activity occurs. The cost to subjects for helping their partners (who were anonymous) changed with each trial. TPJ neural activity was strongly active when participants faced a tough choice—to act altruistically but at a high personal cost.

In another study, subjects were told the money would be withdrawn from their bank accounts and donated to charities. Subjects could also willingly donate to a charity. Brain activity was monitored during both situations. When subjects had no choice to give or withhold money to charities, TPJs still lit up on MRIs from the pleasure of giving. If the giving was by free will, brain activity lit up brightest, and pleasurable feelings were at the highest level.[**]

So, it is normal for Homo sapiens to expect fairness. Those who make us happier by their sacrificial kindnesses also make themselves happy. Who wouldn't want to work in an environment with a fair and selfless boss? We are going to find out how these qualities factor into engagement. We will also look at environments run by the apathetic. No one is happy there, not even the selfish ones. Their TPJs don't light up from altruistic behavior. There isn't any.

The *Smart* Chemicals

> Let's peek inside an engaged brain … When people are passionate about their work, they look for new challenges, new learning, whatever it takes to do what they do better. As all of this happens, dopamine is released.

[**] Readers can review these studies online:
http://www.brainhealthandpuzzles.com/brain_effects_of_altruism.html;

http://www.huffingtonpost.com/2012/07/19/altriusm-brain-temporoparietaljunction_n_1679766.html;

http://www.psmag.com/culture-society/scientists-locate-brains-altruism-center-43356/.

Dopamine is the reward and pleasure chemical, but it is also responsible for creating new learning pathways.

Now, let's say someone recognizes your efforts—maybe a handwritten note from your boss or a colleague saying, *"Hey way to go,"* or, *"Thanks for your help on that project"*—the brain releases a chaser of serotonin. Serotonin is another *"feel good"* chemical that stimulates the *"thinking brain"* and is largely responsible for overall emotional well-being.

According to the 2017 SHRM Job Satisfaction Survey, of the top contributing factors to job satisfaction, three are emotional: respectful treatment, trust, and feeling valued as a member of the team. These emotional factors—when present—release oxytocin. Oxytocin is released when we feel connected, a sense of belonging, safe, and accepted. Because we are wired to connect with others, oxytocin is essential to emotional safety. All three of these chemicals—oxytocin, serotonin, and dopamine—stimulate activity in the prefrontal cortex, or the thinking brain. This is the part of the brain that does the heavy lifting with planning, problem-solving, decision-making, impulse control, and creativity.

The *Stress* Chemical (cue the ominous music): The brain is all about safety first—and not just physical safety, but emotional safety, too. In order to survive when any kind of threat and fear are present, the brain will focus on safety and survival and hold off on any new learning. To the brain, work-related stress is a threat.

When we experience work-related stress, the resources that could be used for new learning are diverted to the part of the brain concerned with survival. At the first sign of danger, cortisol is released and activates the survival brain. Because the brain is so incredibly efficient, it shuts down the production of all of those good chemicals and puts the thinking brain on hold to go deal with the threat in the survival brain.

Neuroscientists have discovered that *"social pain"* or emotional pain activates the same brain regions as physical pain. The researchers also found that witnessing the social pain of another person activated a similar physical pain response in the bystander. People in the workplace become entwined with your sense of self at a neural level. Their fear/threat response becomes yours and yours becomes theirs. Emotional contagion is powerful. Numerous surveys indicate that job stress is a pervasive problem. And all that stress is putting a lot of *thinking brains* on hold!

Melissa Hughes, PhD, 2020: https://info.melissahughes. rocks/neuronugget/inside-the-brains-of-engaged-employees-1

5

SUPER-MOTIVATOR: INSIDE JOB

Most people aren't anywhere near to realizing their creative potential, in part because they're laboring in environments that impede intrinsic motivation.

—TERESA AMABILE

Factoid: Unengaged and disengaged people get the same salary as engaged people. They have no monetary reason to be engaged.

B︎UT WAIT A SEC! EXPENDING extra effort *without pay* is normal. Like in the gym, doing crossword puzzles, painting pictures, building things, working in our gardens. We do it because we *want* to. Enjoyment, challenge, achievement, competition and pride drive us. The rewards are different in kind. Feeling satisfied after a salary raise is transient. Relieving someone's misery, achieving a tough goal, or creating something beautiful gives lasting satisfaction. Self-concept and self-esteem rise. We relish those good feelings.

That's the world of intrinsic intangibles. Elusive as they are to measure, their driving power on productivity far exceeds that of the tangibles.

Yet, of the eighteen benefits listed in chapter 1's table, only two intrinsic needs are partially satisfied: "Flextime" and "work-from-home" options grant some autonomy, an intrinsic motivator. "Promote from within" supports another, advancement.

Factoid: The penny in the corporate bubble gum machine is stuck. Six of eight intrinsic motivators are still begging for attention; the machine needs a good shake.

Ahead, readers will learn about all eight extrinsic work motivators plus eight intrinsic work motivators (The Smart16). But let's summarize the findings thus far that matter. Metrics and analytics must point to causes and effects. Note that these findings are similar to the models of Maslow, McGregor, and Herzberg. Yet those scholars did not connect the dots to actual profits—the effects. Our approach here includes calculations showing direct causality between specific intangibles and profits—to the dollar (if readers can fathom that). So, let's review what we know so far and drop in a few things we'll soon learn.

1. Management focuses on extrinsic motivators. Strong correlations between extrinsic satisfaction and engagement are nonexistent. Extrinsic motivators can retard performance; their range of effectiveness is finite. Conversely, intrinsic satisfaction and engagement strongly correlate.
2. Extrinsic motivators make us work to satisfy our basic needs. When satisfied, our complaining stops, but it doesn't bring us job satisfaction (Frederick Herzberg nailed it).
3. Intrinsic motivators are intangible reasons to expend extra effort. Enjoyment, challenge, purpose, achievement, pride, recognition, status, and progress toward life goals engage us. Output, in pursuit of these through our jobs, is far higher.
4. When our tasks match our interests and utilize our best skills, intrinsic motivators are activated. They are the gold mines! Extrinsic motivators can't trigger creativity. Failure to maximize

intrinsic motivators shows insufficient thought has gone into strategic people priorities.

5. Executives don't manage how their managers handle their staffs' work needs. That fact alone sacrifices control of engagement.

If you're a C-suite resident, you know that executives' decisions since 1850 didn't engage workforces. You know that forfeited profits. You know most of your managers are not going the extra mile to meet their people's needs. You now know that the lack of discretionary effort is normal due to this endemic default.

We are one species with common work needs.

Factoid: We now know what motivates us—satisfying intrinsic needs. We failed to motivate others because we didn't offer them what we were looking for.

Inaction on all work needs and their satisfiers keeps the windfall out of reach. *The Extra-Mile Manager* obviates reasons and excuses for unengaged associates. Knowing these, Readers can develop motivated people who exude black ink. Assessment and development of *extra-mile management behavior* is the only human productivity strategy that is proven to yield ROI.

My Employee Experience

Leaving a good job that I loved was a hard thing. I had been inventory controller for Toyota South Africa at their Prospection assembly plant, south of Durban, for three and a half years. It should have never come to this point.

A department re-org put me under a different boss, one new to the company. I was not happy. I loved my last boss. He was fair and considerate. All I did for the next two months was train my new boss about what we were doing and how we did it. After that, the CFO put an assignment on him that he couldn't handle—prepare an engine-parts reject report for accounting so they could bill Japan for wasted labor and acquire replacement parts.

Engine plant management and staff were under great duress to keep the assembly lines running. Keeping track of defective parts wasn't on anyone's priority list. People were too stressed to care, even if they wanted to. Hundreds of parts were strewn along walls in no order and without identifying tags. The salvage department also had defective parts for minor repairs and reinspection. No one available had any idea what to count as what, or how to estimate wasted labor on engines and components that failed stress tests on the benches.

Engine plant managers chased my new boss out of there. So, he sent me in. I knew their situation. He expected me to produce a chart full of part numbers, descriptions, and quantities with no help from engineers or technicians. He simply needed someone to blame for what he couldn't do. I knew the outcome before I reached the engine plant. The mere sight of me talking to someone sent a manager straight for me. The person I was talking to ran off.

I reported the experience to my new boss. His response: "So you managed to turn the engine plant against the supplies department, and you're telling me you can't carry out a simple instruction! Why do we need you?"

Better wasn't within, so better couldn't come out. Thoroughly disgusted, I went to his boss, who said he would talk to him. It wouldn't matter. The man lacked integrity and wasn't worthy of respect. I had been firing on intrinsic motivators for over three years. I hit the bottom of Maslow's pyramid on the spot. With a wife and three kids relying on me, and now no job, I had to eat this experience and rebound asap. Easy enough to say.

6

SURVIVE OR FLOURISH

All men seek to rule, but if they cannot
rule, they prefer to be equal.

—BRIAN KLAAS

Needs-equity levels the playing field at work. So, are you thinking it's time to nail down these work needs? You got it right. Thanks for your concentration as we prepared the stage for this.

Management doesn't have to be perfect (thankfully). Associates aren't. Their perceptions of their bosses improve when their work needs are satisfied at least 80 percent of the time. At that metric, they feel their leaders are going the extra mile for them. Staffs' adversaries are bosses preoccupied with their own agendas. Any names or faces come to mind? Sometimes it's the one in our mirror. If so, cheer up; 80 percent is within reach.

> *Factoid: If our staff needs it to function, and we could give*
> *it but don't, we are dysfunctional.*

Precisely what does all staff need and desire? The need to survive and the desire to flourish. Survival requires air, water, and food. We also need protection from the elements and hostile animals (including Homo sapiens). To meet these needs, outside sources are required. So, we call them extrinsic needs or motivators. (See table left.)

Extrinsic Motivators: I need to...
1. Be treated fairly and equally with others.
2. Have my group's acceptance.
3. Have the necessary tools, resources, information, and instructions to do my job.
4. Be trusted to do good work.
5. Always know what my boss expects from me.
6. Have a supportive boss who helps solve problems that affect me.
7. Have my work unit/department be well organized.
8. Receive good pay and benefits, and to be given fair evaluations of my performance.

Infants are dependent on external providers, initially parents, who care for them through childhood and adolescence. Yet the need for such care continues into adulthood. We're made that way. Extrinsic needs include a range of work needs. Providers switch to managers—and it's showtime! The macro behavior to satisfy extrinsic needs is nurturing, a repertoire of competencies. This primal behavior with kids and spouses at home declines sharply at work, where staff is non-kin. At work, many extrinsic needs go begging. Gaps must be measured and closed. The Smart16 Survey (discussed later) makes that happen.

Intrinsic motivators (see table opposite page) concern flourishing. They aren't biologically or security-based. Rather, they are psychological. Flourishing is personally growing, having and fulfilling high aspirations; using one's best talents; and attaining recognition and higher status. The macro-behavior that satisfies intrinsic needs is, of course, leadership—also a repertoire of competencies.

Leaders take their teams to better psychological—more stimulating, more fulfilling, idyllic—places. They set challenges, give growth opportunities, and broaden the scope and magnitude of possibilities. These ignite staff motivators. This is every manager's daily, hot investment opportunity.

Factoid: Clients do not come first. Employees come first. If you take care of your employees. they will take care of the clients. (Richard Branson)

Intrinsic Motivators: I desire to …
9. Have work that interests me, challenges me, and utilizes my best skills.
10. Grow my competencies, knowledge, skills, and experience through my job.
11. Have the autonomy and authority to perform my job as I think best.
12. Know that my work is contributing to the organization's goals.
13. Receive recognition and rewards for my performance.
14. Relate well with my colleagues and have their respect.
15. Participate in decisions and have my suggestions valued.
16. Have the opportunity to advance and to achieve my life's purpose.

Earlier pioneers' studies, plus findings presented here, led to The Smart16. Items 4, 11, and 14 are cited by other writers, including myself, as strong motivators. Edward Deci and Richard Ryan (Self-Determination Theory, SDT)[*] correlated satisfaction of these with staffs' performance evaluations. Numbers 2, 8, 13, and 16 are similar to Maslow's basic or higher needs. Number 15 is a Macgregor Y-style motivator. Herzberg would classify number 5 as a hygiene factor and 9 as a satisfier (motivator). Notice that closely associated needs are combined for brevity.

Responses from over 10,000 Smart16 Surveys on numbers 1, 3, 6, 7, 10, and 12 yielded 60,000 data bits for analysis (330,000 bits from the thirty-three survey questions). Satisfaction of these needs (in four countries/cultures) correlates highly with declining productivity indexes (chapter 9).

The numerical balance (extrinsic/intrinsic) is bilaterally balanced, a curiosity (the brain's two hemispheres?) worthy of others' study. Of course, satisfiers derive from only two sources—others or the nature of the work. Maslow concluded that aspirations (intrinsic desires) emerge

---

[*] Richard Ryan and Edward Deci, *Self-Determination Theory: Basic Psychological Needs in Motivation, Development and Wellness* (Guilford Press, 2016).

when necessities (extrinsic needs) have been satisfied. We found that intrinsic satisfiers increase individual and team productivity, though some extrinsic needs are as yet unsatisfied.

The Employee Experience

As of this writing, Vladimir Putin's army has invaded and is shelling Ukraine. Reports are that he has fired five generals. According to captured Russian soldiers, they came for "training exercises," not to kill neighboring Ukrainian civilians. Some became so averse to the mission that they punctured holes in the gas tanks of their tanks or trucks and abandoned them. Ruthless, lying, manipulative bosses made expensive blunders. Soldiers' needs were ignored. They negatively reciprocated with active disengagement—sabotage!

When leaders are tyrannical, people take great risks to escape them or bring them down. The nonobvious is the road less traveled. Those who choose to stay on the beaten path decline a nobler option. Metrics will remind them of that. Unsatisfied needs predict such managers will not bring intangibles, and the profit they can generate, under control. It seems intuitive that 68 percent of the staff is unengaged because 75 percent of intrinsic motivators are unsatisfied. Factually, our human condition forestalls behavioral modification. But it's a surmountable issue. We modify our behaviors when it is strongly in our interest. We have identified that interest. It drives the solution.

Readers who took high school chemistry may have learned that dropping a pea-sized piece of sodium or potassium into a basin of water makes it sizzle and then explode two seconds later. But if we drop the average manager into a new work group, who can predict what will happen? Which of the manager's behaviors will elicit positive responses from the staff? Shouldn't we know?

The Extra Mile Manager is our quest for bedrock truths. For example, *the high level of care a manager takes to ensure the team has what it needs is the strongest predictor of the team's performance.* The converse (where two thirds are unengaged) is our inveterate bugbear.

In many cases, there is a darker intangible reason why staffs' work needs are denied. We pointed out managers who are absorbed in their own agendas. For some, that agenda includes the misuse of power. Once a corruptible manager obtains it, staff needs may not only be ignored, staff may become victims of very sinister behaviors.

The Employee Experience

When psychopathy is sampled in society as a whole, about one in every five hundred people scores above the psychopath threshold of thirty. In the study of aspiring corporate managers, it was one in every twenty-five. Those results could be an outlier, but that study suggests that there are about twenty times more psychopaths in corporate leadership than in the general population. (Other studies have suggested that one in a hundred are psychopaths, suggesting a fourfold over-representation in corporate leadership.) Most intriguing of all, seven of the nine subjects who scored above a twenty-five, "two were vice-presidents, two were directors, two were managers or supervisors, and one held some other management position." (Brian Klaas, *Corruptible: Who Gets Power and How It Changes Us*)

Who disagrees that change is needed when employees cringe under insipid or overbearing leaders? But when it involves the ethics and characters of bosses, we are less comfortable imposing standards to control them. Codes of conduct, sexual harassment laws, and equal employment legislation control prejudicial, offensive, and unfair treatment. As long as owners and their managers don't violate such codes and laws, we leave them alone.

But what about higher principles impacting feelings and mental health that are willfully ignored with no intervention? A manager may rant at staff in the confines of his or her department, wounding feelings at will, but if the department next door doesn't overhear and report it, the only consequence is buried in a turnover statistic and a tinge of red ink on the balance sheet. When abusers get away with it, they are not shy to do whatever at anyone's expense. That's attracting focus.

7

CAUSATION VERSUS CORRELATION

Effective leaders who understand the correlation between higher levels of engagement, happiness, and productivity facilitate movement in the right direction—and have people feel good about it.

—POLL, PARTNERS IN LEADERSHIP

Readers, would statistical correlations between intangible inputs and profits help us control the relevant inputs? You're probably thinking *yes,* but have you ever had them to rely on? In the above quotation, *"leaders who understand the correlation"* are acknowledging that a likely cause-effect relationship exists. That's not exactly proven mathematical probability. Statistical validity is a higher bar of certitude. We need that higher certainty to stop living on the hope that our leadership training will stick on the job. Any firm replicating the conditions in our studies can predict and document ROI from institutionalized work needs-equity.

From the outset (by my revised job assignment at Beares), the validity route was chosen for me. To attain it, two variables had to be identified: work needs and the management behaviors that satisfy them. Why work needs? They concern motivation. The quest to satisfy needs and desires drives behavior. The next step was correlating work need satisfaction with higher productivity. Of course, higher productivity correlates 1:1 with higher profit. Rising levels of satisfaction hinge on managers' behavioral changes. These hinge on measurement, feedback, accountability and training. To complete the validity process for ROI, the following thesis had to be proven. It required audited financial statements for three consecutive years from the implementation of tools—each study's launch point:

> Thesis: Over time, rising levels of human productivity will lower the ratio of payroll costs to revenues. That will raise profit. Productivity will rise when work needs are satisfied at a high level. Work needs will be satisfied when managers are made accountable and trained to satisfy them.

The ratio of payroll to revenues declines when more work gets done by the same number of people. Or the same revenues are attained with fewer people. Staff that leaves may not need to be replaced. Retrenchment is unnecessary. Revenues rise when the sales and support departments are more productive thanks to better-satisfied work needs.

I imagine readers are wondering, *what level of mathematical probability can be relied on?* The minimum statistic we attributed as strongly causal was $r = 0.70$. The highest r attained in one study was 0.86. In simple terms, the lower r number means there was a 70 percent chance that the independent variable (IV) caused the dependent variable (DV) and a 30 percent chance it did not. The 40 percent differential is a strong indicator of cause. At $r = 0.86$, there is only a 14 percent chance that the IV did not cause the DV. The midpoint between these two stats is $r = 0.78$, only a 22 percent chance that the IV being tested did not change the DV being measured. Statistically insignificant IVs account for the gaps between 1:1 and 1:0.70 and between 1:1 and 1:0.86.

This level of reliability is essential for formulating financial projections and for evidence-based human productivity strategies. The targeted variables were always rising need satisfaction versus declining productivity indexes. While these results stand alone, they are augmented by the effects of senior managers' behavioral changes on the behaviors of their direct reports. We also discovered that a few managers coached their staff on how to respond to the survey. Need satisfaction scores were high, but PI scores were not predictably declining. The research partner firm replaced the managers. Future scores under new managers showed declining departmental productivity indexes by the next year.

Because behavioral change is gradual, studies need sufficient time for that change to be noticeable in statistics. ROI will peak after three consecutive years of institutionalized work need satisfaction. Vendor programs that don't statistically verify ROI are well-intentioned but speculative. So how are capital expenditure decisions being made for management/leadership training?

Vendors present client lists of notable firms that acquired their programs. They cite overwhelming evidence from workshop participant evaluations on how well the training was received. They cite testimonials from training participants and decision-makers on the perceived positive effects of the program. The inference is, *all of these people can't be wrong.* In essence, the *evidence* is largely anecdotal.

When we purchase a multi-million-dollar machine to increase productivity, the evidence for that decision is prima facie. Past purchasers have documented evidence of productivity before and after their purchases. Capital expenditures need evidentiary justification. Or we gamble capital.

With 68 percent unengaged in the United States (and dismal globally) before buying or renewing programs to address the un-engagement issue, let's contrast Firm A with Firm B.

Firm A: Without Needs-Equity

This firm does not manage how its managers manage their people. The absence of validated instruments for increasing productivity and profit through needs-equity leaves firms vulnerable to negative intangibles. Random behaviors include many that erode profit by raising costs. Such behaviors correlate with lower engagement and higher productivity indexes. Firm A's characteristics:

- Managers' job descriptions have no requirement for work-need satisfaction.
- Managers may not care what their staff thinks of them.
- Managers' unbridled, offensive behaviors may be on display without consequences.
- Management does not permit staff to evaluate their managers' behavior toward them.
- Managers have favorites and neglect staff that aren't favored.
- Staff has little recourse for unfairness, rudeness, apathy and discrimination.
- Managers can rule by fear or threat, largely ignore staff, or micromanage them.
- Staff needs for tools, information, instruction, guidance, and support may go unsatisfied.
- Managers may not enrich staff jobs, develop them or recognize their contributions.
- Staff turnover, disengagement, and disharmony are tolerated or go unnoticed and unmeasured.
- Human productivity from intangible sources (payroll ÷ revenues) is not a monitored statistic.

Such conditions create large gaps between what people *want* versus their reality. These gaps disgruntle staff and cause un-engagement and turnover. Tolerating them, normal in most firms, increases labor costs and reduces profit (evidence of problem). Staff has no voice heard loudly enough to evoke change. Managers get a pass. Unmet work needs are not on senior management's agendas.

Firm B: With Needs-Equity

This firm manages how its managers manage their people. It operates under a validated program that increases productivity and profit from positive intangibles (leadership and nurturing vis-à-vis work needs). Strategic behaviors are developed and applied. Random behaviors are curtailed. Positive behaviors correlate with high engagement and low productivity indexes. Firm B's Characteristics:

- Managers' job descriptions require work-need satisfaction at 80 percent level or above.
- Managers care what staff thinks of them. Metrics incentivize caring.
- Management asks staff to periodically evaluate their managers' behaviors toward them.
- Staff reports on unfairness, rudeness, apathy, and discrimination through a survey instrument.
- Managers who incite fear, threaten, ignore staff, or micromanage are spotlighted.
- Staffs' needs for tools, information, instruction, guidance and support are well satisfied.
- Managers enrich staff jobs, develop staff and recognize staff contributions.
- Turnover, disengagement and conflict are measured. Improvement strategies are applied.
- Monitoring departments' productivity indices is an institutionalized practice.

Such behaviors and strategies narrow or close *want versus is* gaps, ingratiate staff, increase engagement, and reduce turnover. Increasing the intensity and frequency of positive behaviors lowers labor costs and raises profits (evidence of solution). Staff voices are heard in the C-suite, where they evoke change. Work needs are on senior management's agenda. No manager gets a pass on inequities in work-need satisfaction.

Readers who opt to replace random negative behaviors with strategic ones will be doing what they were hired to do—take good care of staff and raise profit from their departments. By confronting the validity issue, we are in a stronger position to advise on development tools and strategies. We all know the effect we want. Using validated tools delivers it. The employee experience of the past need not be the employee experience of the future. Future staff work experiences are financially pivotal. Output soars when staff jobs are fulfilling. It's basic: Staff reports work-need gaps via the Smart16 Survey. Their managers get custom strategies to close the gaps. Applying them is part of their job. Productivity rises.

As readers discover in chapter 8, a law of nature waits for us to take initiative. When we do the right thing *first*, nature shows its appreciation. Lead and nurture as needs require. Nice statistics necessarily ensue.

8

RECIPROCITY: WHAT'S YOUR FLAVOR?

*Giving is better than receiving because
giving starts the receiving process.*

—JIM ROHM

Extrinsic motivators must be met, but satisfying them doesn't drive performance. Intrinsic motivators do that. These have two aspects: what the job gives associates (challenge, growth, achievement, recognition, a sense of worth, and fulfillment); what the manager gives associates (caring attention for their range of work desires). This "care" is the leadership macro skill tabled in chapter 6. Desires are about something better. Effective leaders take us to that place.

What compels associates to positively respond to work-need satisfaction? Studies in social anthropology delivered the answer. Our task was to prove it works in business. It is the...

Social Law of Reciprocity

When someone does something nice for you, you will have a deep-rooted psychological urge to do something nice in return. As a matter of fact, you may even reciprocate with a gesture far more generous than their original good deed.

Language expresses this universal phenomenon. It has two flavors: Take care of staff's work needs and they will positively reciprocate. Diminish them or ignore their needs, and they will negatively reciprocate.

POSITIVE RECIPROCITY	NEGATIVE RECIPROCITY
You scratch my back, I'll scratch yours	Blow for blow
Win-win	Reap what you sow
Give and take	What goes around comes around
Do for others what you wish them to do for you	Sow the wind, reap the whirlwind
One hand washes the other	Chickens come home to roost
Return a favor	Tit for tat
Quid pro quo	Eye for an eye, tooth for a tooth

These behaviors exist between individuals, between groups and between nations. Many species exhibit reciprocal behaviors. It fosters cooperation, censure or withdrawal from relationships. What are the business versions of it that affect productivity?

Factoid: Disengagement is mental resignation (withdrawal). Active disengagement is negative reciprocity (spite). Engagement is a combination of positive reciprocity and intrinsic motivation.

In 2004, Krueger and Mas[*] showed that defective tires at the Decatur Firestone/Bridgestone plant increased amid labor/management disputes. Employees went on strike for better treatment. The company's tires were failing on Ford Explorers fitted with them. Rollovers took 101 lives. Replacement staff for strikers included members of management. Product quality suffered due to managers' inexperience with production equipment, plus hostile relations with factory staff. Negative reciprocity went public.

Conversely, positive reciprocity from equitable treatment is a corporate asset. But it's not real until corporations create it. Until then, between two-thirds

---

[*] https://www.nber.org/papers/w9524

and four-fifths unengaged or disengaged is the response to unsatisfied, but crucial work needs. People even negatively or positively reciprocate on behalf of others they identify with; it's called *indirect reciprocity*. Entire groups may push back on management as in the case above.

Reciprocity's positive flavor emerges after firms adopt and institutionalize needs-parity between management and staff. Parity (equity) must be a cultural value for the 16 needs and desires tabled in chapter 6. Job descriptions assign accountability to meet them. Programs drill it in as policy. Sustainability requires these actions. Line and staff managers are the initiators. Failure to elicit positive reciprocity is a failure to manage productivity, a status quo vote, and a drain on profit.

Many of us have read the claim, "our people are our greatest asset" in lobby mission statements, but they bear little alignment with a high percentage of disengaged staff. "We go the extra mile for our greatest asset," if claimed and supported, would show a majority of people engaged if Gallup, Inc. knocked on the door for metrics.

It seems that negative reciprocity is not a high concern in the C-suite. There's no system to avert it. Execs may not like their latest climate survey. But, they can't tell you their productivity index (PI) for last month. Who has a plausible guess about how much more profit would accrue if engagement were 90 percent? CFOs might consider the Third Bucket of Profit (PI). Normally, the focus doesn't get past buckets 1 and 2—gross margin and expense control. But without hard data to propel change, we trek on as I did before Mr. Rogoff put his finger on behavioral ROI.

> *Factoid: US Department of Labor statistics show that the number one reason people leave is because they don't feel appreciated.*

People feel appreciated when managers give them what they need (Intrinsic 13). To get a handle on and control the PI, I modified the Department of Labor's formula as follows: \$Payroll ÷ \$Revenues = PI. Work unit, department, and corporate productivity are all measured by the PI. Under this formula, a low PI means high profit. That is because a lower ratio of payroll costs to revenues means higher profit.

Productivity Index:
Ratio of Payroll Costs To Revenues

Net Profit

PI fluctuates relative to associates' and managers' outputs. Higher outputs across an organization raise revenues. Existing staff, when engaged, raise outputs. If an associate leaves, he or she may not need to be replaced. Payroll costs decline. Profit rises.

Intangibles have been the bane of executives for one reason: In dialogue about staff productivity, often the last issue discussed—if at all—is what associates want from the boss and the job. We made that faux pas at Beares. At that stage, the faux pas was universal. Needs-parity dispels that costly oversight and its downside.

> *Factoid: If one expects ROI, one must distinguish between intangible entities that yield a return and intangible entities that don't.*

As the remedy for engaging people is implemented, managers invest more time and effort in staff. Staff transitions from disengaged to un-engaged to engaged. Staffs feel their managers' care. Opinions of managers transform over time from self-absorbed to accommodating to caring and inspiring. Positive reciprocity comes into play. Intangible assets rise in value.

Pushback dissipates. When bosses ask for "all in" to meet a deadline, they get it. When a firm creates positive reciprocity but its competitors don't, that firm produces and delivers at a lower cost and with higher quality and better service. The social law of reciprocity, for so long delivering the wrong flavor, now works for the firm. On the extra mile, good deeds are rewarded.

Our work with clients, domestic and abroad, revealed that three out of twenty staff are incorrigible free riders. They like getting; giving, not so much. The social law of reciprocity has sanctions for violators; they lose favor. Reciprocity from the group is negative; it is felt and has its way. Free riders move on to more permissive, laissez-faire environs.

That said, it is easy for a work need to be overlooked, which the reader has observed on this quest. Weak hands needed bigger rubber bands. Weak arms needed someone else to make the coffee.

My Employee Experience

At age fourteen, I got a job waiting on counter customers in a diner on Glenarm Street in downtown Denver. Coffee was drawn from a large urn sitting on the backbar. Three gallons could be made from a pound of coffee grounds poured into a filter at the top of the urn. The center spigot on the urn would yield three gallons of hot water at just below the boiling point. I had never made coffee. The adult waitresses or the manager made it. They would lift three gallons of water, one by one, to the top of the urn and then pour each into the filter. Pretty simple.

I was a little over five feet tall at the time. The waitresses were busy, and the manager told me to make coffee. Lifting the gallon over my head wasn't easy. As I raised it unsteadily to the top of the urn to tilt it into the filter it bumped the top of the urn and hot water poured over my right hand. I couldn't set it down quickly enough so I could head for the restroom. It was occupied. By the time I got inside, my hand was blistered from my fingers to my wrist.

I caught a bus from downtown to a doctor out on East Colfax. The doc cut away the blistered skin and then put on ointment and a bandage. I was off for two weeks without pay. I had tried to do a task, as instructed, that I was unable to do without risk. Over the years, the scars mostly faded away.

An old nursery rhyme comes to mind:

> I do it normal,
> I do it slow.
> You do it with me,
> then off you go.

As readers recall, we never know when a staff member's need may pop up just like a customer's need. In some cases that calls for a little on-the-spot caring.

Are you ready to measure the impact on productivity from more frequent leadership behaviors that fire up intrinsic motivators? Managing productivity metrics is a major good deed. We'll do the math at your pace.

9

PRODUCTIVITY INDEX: THE THIRD BUCKET OF PROFIT

Four out of three people struggle with math.

—T-SHIRT MESSAGE

CONTROLLING ENGAGEMENT ISN'T POSSIBLE IF we don't do engagement's math. That means calculating the exact financial impact of intangible inputs. If you are ready, let's put on our accounting hats and get started. We will leverage our managers' behaviors, to their benefit, to positively change our firms' bottom lines.

Executives who say, "Productivity is our competitive advantage," but have a financial ailment from unhappy people, contradict the evidence. When we look at labor costs and ask, *"what are we getting for our money?"* that's about the ratio of payroll to revenues. If it's high, the firm has an ailment. If it's optimal (like 98.6° body temp) the firm is healthy.

The PI measures financial consequences from the intangible realm. Knowing and controlling what affects the PI is extra-mile due diligence. Those who don't control this metric know much less about their businesses than they think. The unorganized nonobvious is biting them at will.

There are two formulas for the PI. The first formula—the universal one—does nothing to improve an organization's health through higher engagement. It focuses on money, not on the motivation of the people who produce it. It divides outputs by inputs. For example:

$40M revenue (output) ÷ $9M payroll (input) = $4.44 revenue (per payroll dollar spent).

Is management strategizing with $4.44 to grow engagement? Instead, the firm's focus is on strategies to raise revenues, like marketing campaigns, higher pricing for products or services, and higher sales targets. Has anyone explained how those strategies engage salespeople?

The perennial misstep is doing everything except making PI the top KPI. Setting higher sales targets cannot be the only gun management fires. The drivers are commissions or bonuses, which raise the cost of sales. There are upper and lower limits to the effectiveness of these incentives. But engagement has no downside or financial cost.

Factoid: Financial strategies that are dependent on people's performances cannot omit what people need to perform.

Fixation on outputs keeps our blinders on. Unless inputs change, outputs are static. Inputs won't change if enough execs keep seeing the $4.44 metric as academic, without benefit or liabillty. In that all-to-common scenario, money keeps silently slipping through the cracks.

Before we get to the second PI formula—the strategic one—let's redeem some value from the $4.44 quotient. It gives us a new quotient we can work with:

1. Convert $4.44 to a decimal. The calculation is: 1 ÷ 4.44 = .225.
2. Convert the decimal to a percentage. Drop the decimal point and add the percentage sign to get 22.5%.
3. State the percentage as a ratio of payroll to revenues: Payroll is 22.5% of revenues.

4. Apply strategies provided in this book to lower that ratio. Every one percent the ratio declines adds one percent of revenues to profit. (That's a lot of money!)

Step 4 raises a question: Will rising and falling PI trends be tracked by department managers? They get a higher salary for what? For leading a productive team. But what if they don't? That's when we put the math to work for us. The second formula identifies the exact payroll investment made by every department and the whole company. To calculate these, we change the dividend to the divisor and vice versa:

$9M (payroll) ÷ $40M (revenue) = .225 or 22.5% of revenues.

The impotent $4.44 is out of the picture. With 22.5 percent in focus, it stands out that payroll is grabbing a big chunk of revenue, leaving less for profit. Managers can focus on how much revenue their departments are grabbing, leaving less for managers' bonuses based on earnings. In simpler terms:

- Some people catch fish (generate revenues).
- Some cut bait (input supporting revenues).
- Cut less bait, catch less fish.
- ROI from payroll tanks.
- Conversely, cut more bait, catch more fish.

The last bullet point means the ratio of payroll to revenues will decline. Keeping inputs (bait cutting) in mind (by our PI formula) ensures everyone's priority list supports sales revenues with engaged teams. Every drop in a department's payroll investment injects black ink on the bottom line. Revenues increase and labor costs decline. How does it work department by department?

- If we satisfy everyone's work needs, especially intrinsic ones that make motivational and creative juices flow, will everyone contribute more to business objectives?

- If our sales managers more effectively lead and support sales teams in their work needs, will the teams write more business?
- If our marketing department has more effective ad campaigns (cuts more bait), will sales go up?
- If our customer service improves, will we retain clients who are more likely to recommend our firm's products and services?
- If the supply chain is more reliable, will timely production and delivery help get repeat business?
- If the finance department handles customer account queries professionally and supports clients through cash flow issues, will that help retain clients and get new ones?

Without dispute, a department's motivation, discretionary effort, creativity, innovation, and collaboration all increase when people's intrinsic motivators are activated. More gets done with fewer payroll costs. Let's make PI our top KPI; it puts people first. Caring drives profit strategy. We'll learn how managers are incentivized to care. The C-suite steps up.

To drill this into our psyches, let's do a little more math. We contrast Companies A and B:

A. This company's managers continue to fire on instincts, which leaves too many work needs out in the cold. Its revenues are $40M and its payroll is $9M. The PI is .225 (22.5 percent of revenues). Let's say the company has been netting 6 percent annually on $40M in revenues: That's $2.4M.

B. This company's managers satisfy people's work needs above the 80 percent level. Department managers raised revenues to $50M, but payroll remained at $9M. Payroll costs dropped to 18 percent of revenues. If payroll had remained at 22.5 percent ($50M × .225) payroll would have been $11.25M; $2.25M was saved by higher productivity. Those savings raised the company's net profit to $4.65M, a 94% increase in net profit with static payroll and no one laid off.

The graph below shows a research partner's declining PI from a benchmark of 0.26 at the inception of the study (2011) to 0.21 at the conclusion of the study in 2014. In percentages, payroll dropped from 26 percent of revenues to 21 percent of revenues over three years.

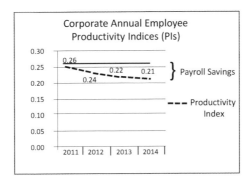

Table 10 shows projected and actual payroll costs based on PI, annual savings, and total new profit accrued from the declining PI on the above graph from 2011 to 2014:

Table 10 *

Year	Benchmark PI	Projected $Payroll	Actual PI	Actual $Payroll	Actual $Savings
2012	.26	$7,510,385	.24	$6,998.561	$511,824
2013	.26	$8,740,849	.22	$7,322,478	$1,418,371
2014	.26	$9,269,227	.21	$7,652,209	$1,617,018
Total		$25,520,461		$21,973,248	**$3,547,213**

Annual Growth in Net Profit %:

2011: Net profit $1,871,079 ÷ Revenue $31,184,650 = 6%

2012: Net profit $2,244,990 ÷ Revenue $28,886,098 = 7.8%

2013: Net profit $3,361,865 ÷ Revenue $33,618,650 = 10%

2014: Net profit $3,756,071 ÷ Revenue $35,650,876 = 10.53%

Annual net profit percentage based on audited accounts. Years 2012 to 2014 based on PI at 26% of revenues. By 2014, payroll savings (column 6) had doubled 2011 net profit to $3,756,071 = 100%.

---

* Table, graph, profit summary excerpted from 2015 study prepared for research partner from audited financial statements.

Unhealthy firms ignore intangibles, reap negative reciprocities and forgo potential profit, there for the taking. For extra-mile managers, behavioral analytics rule—a cause for joy, not grief.

But ignore PI, and the financial ailment is chronic. The answer is a system (box of tools used in the previous study) to institutionalize need satisfaction. Behavioral change is nudged along by accountability and reinforcement.

With the system, firms control worthwhile outcomes from intangible inputs. Note that rising work-need satisfaction from increased frequency of leadership and nurturing behaviors produced a "to-the-dollar profit figure" as promised.

> *Factoid: Money paid to unengaged staff is a cost. When we activate the motivators that engage them, the cost converts to an investment with a measurable return.*

Monitoring and controlling your PI fills The Third Bucket of Profit. Gross margin and expense control (buckets 1 and 2) are usually already optimized. The untapped windfall is in bucket 3. Do the math. If not, un-engagement and losses persist, as these reality checks attest.

The Employee Experience

$160,000. That's the extra annual cost in dollars for managing just one nasty leader who indulges in personal insults, sarcastic jokes, withering emails, and other displays of hostile behavior. Besides extracting a significant financial toll—such as the cost of anger management or other counseling, settling litigation by victims, and reorganizing departments or teams— workplace bullies inflict considerable human damage, driving employees out of organizations and increasing anxiety, stress, and burnout among those who remain. As they move up the corporate ladder, senior executives run the risk of becoming insensitive and unkind to others. (McKinsey and Company, "Leading Off," 2022)

Three out of four working Americans say their boss is the most stressful part of their job—44% say they've been verbally, emotionally, or physically abused by a supervisor or boss at some point in their career, and 31% of workers say their boss just doesn't appreciate them. Sounds like a big group of whiners, doesn't it? Actually, employees with subpar management have the right to complain—and this dissatisfaction is costing businesses and the American economy big money.

1. The Economy: Bad working relationships between management and employees costs the economy $360 billion each year from lost productivity. Fake sick days, dawdling because of low-motivation, and purposefully making mistakes out of spite are all direct results of a bad boss—and it costs the economy big bucks.

2. Health is at Stake: Anyone who has ever had a bad boss knows they can't just shake them off when they turn in their two weeks' notice. In fact, it takes people 22 months to restore their stress levels to a healthy range after a bout of "terrible boss". Also, people who are stuck working for someone horrible are more susceptible to chronic stress, depression, and anxiety—which all increase the risk of a lowered immune system, colds, strokes, and even heart attacks. All those sick days and visits to the doctor, acupuncturist, massage therapist, and psychologist are costing companies a pretty penny in health costs and lost work days.

3. Last but not least, a bad boss produces some very real costs in the form of recruitment costs, lost productivity during new-hire training, and in cases that escalate—legal fees. One organization who did the math on real money lost in a year because of one boss's bad repertoire with employees added up a whopping $160,000— well above the average managerial salary in many industries. (https://www.onlinemba.com/blog/true-cost-bad-boss/)

Really, Friends? We've been trying to cure disengagement without caring about people.

10

GAPS GALORE

There are no traffic jams along the extra mile.

—ROGER STAUBACH

WHAT WE DON'T YET KNOW about the 16 extrinsic and intrinsic motivators is who feels strongly about one or more in particular right now. Nor do we know how often these feelings are manifesting. So extra-mile managers put the Smart16 Survey to work. It probes all needs/desires at intervals. The point is to match satisfaction strategies to current work needs. The manager's coaching report, generated from the survey, provides strategies. Each shrinks or closes a gap.

> *Factoid: The alternative to using a precision tool is everyone's best guess on who needs what and when.*

Organizations have largely been ignoring or winging this. They could, however, have a positive impact by using an accurate tool. The survey has positive and negative statements. Similar to this negative example:

> *I get blindsided by unannounced changes that affect me.*

Readers may say, "Why measure this? Changes are normal." True, to a point. Such a statement is unlikely to be surveyed in other tools, but associates are aggravated by frequent changes. The less-organized or experienced a firm and its managers are, the more changes tumble down on people. Trial-and-error businesses, and their managers, unsettle people. If someone is a change maestro, staff will soon be on to him or her. And they are not neutral.

For the blindsided example, each staff member selects one of four options: totally agree, agree, disagree, totally disagree. The most favorable response is the norm. In this case, it's "totally disagree." Any other response is a deviation (variance) from that norm. Variances are gaps in satisfaction. The survey measures three sigmas of variance. When three sigmas manifest, it's a big gap with big downside consequences.

Factoid: The 68 percent of associates who are unengaged have second place all sewed up if their needs and their boss's needs are at odds.

If clicked on, "Totally Agree" would reveal a three-sigma variance and its effect—strong disgruntlement over disruptions from changes. A drop of red ink has started its trip to the bottom line.

A decrease in the intensity of unannounced changes by the next survey is the manager's charge. A machine-learning algorithm populates manager's coaching reports with targeted strategies. These enable chains of command to precisely coach and support application.

We also had to know why vendor leadership training was not transferring to the job. As the reasons became apparent, it meant creating a new pedagogy for developing managers and supervisors. Chapters 22 and 23 cover the perennial issue of poor transference. And of course, the solutions engineered over the course of these studies.

The frequency of feelings must also be measured. How often are associates blindsided by changes? If it's rare, concern is obviated. Staff responses to blindsided frequency were *seldom, sometimes, often,* or *always.* If often is chosen, it's a two-sigma gap from the norm—seldom. The manager's coaching report generates gap-closing strategies:

- Intercept changes before staff is affected.
- Be a buffer on impacts outside your unit's control.
- Solicit staff ideas on the best ways to implement changes.
- Lead/nurture staff through changes to maintain composure and productivity.

Generalities don't work here. Specificity is crucial. Let's say a boss quelled the intensity and frequency of disruptive changes. That drop of red ink aborts its trip and waves on a black drop. That manager didn't have to step up for staff, and many wouldn't have; they have personal agendas to attend to. But in the eyes of this staff, their boss cared enough to go the extra mile. And he or she knew precisely what to do. Would staff feel an urge to step-up if their manager needed some positive reciprocity? More likely than not. Two or three turned-on staff fire up others. Sports matches often hinge one player's outstanding feat.

Sixteen of the survey's thirty-three statements measure the intensity of feelings on unmet needs. Similarly, sixteen measure the frequency of feelings on unmet needs. Gaps appear on many statements. Managers finally know where they fall short and what to do about it. For the first time, there is a sense that engagement can be brought under control. One question allows staff to vent feelings across the spectrum of needs and desires. Managers who satisfied work needs at the 80 percent level or above, plus those who got closer to 80 percent since the previous survey, are recognized.

> *Factoid: When needs–equity drives productivity strategy, staff psychology gets a makeover.*

Intensity gaps display as red ink, or a hue of red, on the manager's coaching report pie charts. Frequency gaps are in red ink, or red hues, on linear graphs (general ledger colors). Charts and graphs without gaps have only black ink. Recognition is due. Increased productivity stemming from managers' actions to satisfy work needs lowers the ratio of payroll to revenues over time. Outputs go up; costs go down. Bottom lines are more strongly in the black.

Red is scary on one's coaching report. It should be. The team has slacked off. But as managers did not know which needs they failed to satisfy, it's development, not confrontation, time. Development is about where we are going (direction) and what our staff needs on the way (support). Leadership and nurturing fill that bill. We all know how to do both—to a degree. We are not starting from scratch. People understand these two roles and that the task is to expand their repertoire of both macro skills by ramping up each's frequency and intensity.

A strong incentive for managers to exhibit prosocial leadership/nurturing behaviors is to avoid appearing selfish or apathetic toward their people when they do not. Survey metrics capture the real-world feelings of the people working for us.

> *Factoid: Sparking more effort from less care is ROI minus the I.*

Strategies to turn red ink to black ink are provided in the manager's coaching reports. These grow managers to 80 percent of perfection and beyond. Given the propensity to selfishness we are born with, 80 percent is stellar. The modules in the virtual university (DiaplanU) also develop need-satisfaction skills using transferable bites to match tasks calling for leadership and/or nurturing. Better metrics, with accompanying rewards, enter the pipeline.

A word about nurturing and leadership: Primal gender differences in behavior are observable. Some males are uncomfortable nurturing other males. Nurturing is more often ascribed to females than males, while leadership is more often ascribed to males than females. It is about our staffs' Smart16 work needs, not our comfort zones. If we overnurture, we increase codependence. If we lead too fast, we leave some people behind. If encouragement, empathy, and sharing of feelings are called for, we give it. If goals and objectives are at stake, we put on our leadership hat, comfortably or not. Chapter 14 offers practice in differentiating macro skill use in various scenarios. It is easy to react istinctively in the trenches. Neural pathways need rewiring to respond appropriately a high percentage of the time. Chapter 25 addresses rewiring.

Having adapted appropriately, should managers rest on their laurels at 20 percent shy of perfect? The second mile is the realm of transformed behaviors. Imperfect people are always adjusting to it. The closer we get to 100 percent, the blacker the ink and the more of it. An intangible caring demeanor incarnates as monetary tangibles through those being cared for.

I came to call engagement management *DIAPLAN*—an acronym for *"Do I Always Provide Leadership And Nurturing?"* It means, whenever they need it, I always provide it. In Spanish, it means *Day Plan*. To lead and nurture is part of every manager's daily plan. Tools and training are in both languages.

The Employee Experience

From executives to supervisors, people who come into power in awful systems are more tempted to be selfish and unempathetic to staff needs. A high percentage of executives have narcissistic, Machiavellian, and psychopathic tendencies ("The Dark Triad"). They tolerate narcissism, apathy, and the negative effects on productivity that these traits engender. Management behavior is shaped by the system. Awful systems don't police managers' behaviors toward staff. Accountability for work-need satisfaction is not part of the culture. The price corporations pay for that is through the roof. (Gleanings from sections of Brian Klaus's book, *Corruptible: Who Gets Power and How It Changes Us*)

11

THE DIRTY DOZEN

*One should never impose one's views on
a problem; one should rather study it, and
in time a solution will reveal itself.*

—ALBERT EINSTEIN

LET'S CONSOLIDATE WHAT WE KNOW so far and what actions can be taken on what we know. Extra-mile managing is an evidence-based strategy. The problem needing a solution? Unengaged people are raising costs and reducing profits. They are unengaged because their jobs, that third of their lives, are not fulfilling. That's not on them. Evidence-based outcomes have two facets:

- ✓ The evidence that identifies *the causes* of a problem.
- ✓ The evidence that identifies *the solutions* to a problem.

We studied the causes of problems in earlier chapters. Chapter 12 sets requirements for effective solutions. Chapter 13 compares extrinsic and intrinsic impacts on solutions. The twelve most prevalent, chronic problems needing solutions are:

The Dirty Dozen

1. Managers' behavior often elicits negative reciprocity from staff. Staff resists, un-engages or disengages.

2. People have 16 work needs. They vary from person to person, time to time. Unmet needs spawn feelings that the boss/company is unconcerned about their needs. Negative feelings retard performance.

3. Managers do not know who needs what or when. They are unable to address many needs. Intrinsic needs (challenge, opportunity, personal growth and recognition) most frequently remain unmet.

4. Payroll costs, relative to revenues, rise when needs are denied. Invariably, needs are denied.

5. The Productivity Index, used by economists/US Dept. of Labor, does not factor in human motivation. Management does not use it to increase work motivation.

6. Many scientists reported the same work motivators, using different models. Yet, no model's use is validated against the Productivity Index (PI). Teaching the models has not changed managers' behavior. There is no accountability for utility or ensuing results.

7. Performance management tools are unvalidated. Performance evaluations are rarely correlated with increased productivity. Evidence is lacking that these boilerplate instruments impact engagement.

8. Managers' job descriptions lack team productivity requirements (to maintain low PIs). Accountability to meet staffs' needs is absent. Competencies that raise staffs' productivity aren't specified.

9. The US spends $166B* annually on leadership training. Yet, the Gallup engagement percent has risen only six percentage points in 21 years. Effort and cost, without results, indicates poor problem identification.

10. CFOs ignore human productivity as a significant source of profit. They manage margins and expenses but have no tools to measure and manage behavioral inputs to profit.

11. Novices are appointed over work groups. It's usually unknown whether they raise or lower team productivity. Companies do not manage how their managers handle their people or their people's needs. Managers' instincts and conditioned behaviors do not adequately serve their staffs' needs.

12. Firms don't institutionalize *caring*. What is institutionalized (normal) is unwitting negligence in staffs' need satisfaction. Unfairness (inequity) engenders resentment and reduces staffs' contribution to business results.

* https://trainingindustry.com/wiki/outsourcing/size-of-training-industry/.

Factoid: In 120 years of management research, motivation issues were not resolved because the methodology didn't raise management's care for the people being studied.

With behavioral change being gradual, studies were time-consuming. In our case, almost four decades working with more than a hundred small to medium-sized firms and many *Fortune* 500 firms. We gathered piecemeal data from firms using our tools in exchange for their data. The first study concluded after seventeen years, another after four years, two others after three years, one following the other. As clarity on cause-effect grew and our technology improved, the time required to institutionalize needs-equity dropped dramatically. Invariably, the root of performance issues was unsatisfied work needs and managers who were oblivious or neglectful of them.

Research drudgery eased as year-to-year need satisfaction survey scores rose in concert with year-to-year declining PIs. Declining PIs were evidence that negative stimuli, which elicited negative responses, were being supplanted by positive stimuli. Managers were opting for purposeful behaviors over random and instinctive behaviors. It was top-down, policy-driven, adaptive behavior. It was nudged along by training and development, focus in meetings, coaching, managerial support, and accountability for rising need satisfaction and declining PIs.

The Employee Experience

Only 17% of employees give their company an exceptional rating for employee experience. And, non-HR employees are twice as likely to rate their company poorly compared with those on the HR team, suggesting a considerable disconnect in perceived employee experience versus reality.

That disconnect means employers aren't delivering an experience that aligns with employees' priorities and motivations as well as they think they are.

Source: Method research article on behalf of Topia: "Adapt or Lose the War for Talent: Why Your Employee Experience Needs an Upgrade."

If an instructional designer can't identify the competencies that satisfy the Smart16, what learning objectives would be the focus of a management curriculum? If training's financial impact can't be measured, it's a fight to keep it in the budget when lean times come.

The remaining chapters in *The Extra Mile Manager* were the most enjoyable to write. Why? Because the rubber meets the road—with success. The dirty dozen sums up the causes. It's time to replace them with leadership and nurturing macro skills and enjoy positive effects.

12

WHY MANAGERS WILL GET IT

We change our behavior when the pain of staying the same becomes greater than the pain of changing.

—HENRY CLOUD

LET'S MOVE FROM CAUSES OF un-engagement to evidence-based solutions that generate engagement. The first step is to understand the requirements for solutions to take hold.

Three factors must be operating for a behavioral solution to take root and drive change:

1. *Awareness:*

   - The firm publishes the needs-equity policy:

     ✓ Citing positive impacts on the firm, its managers and staff from work needs equity,
     ✓ Versus unfavorable impacts from departments with work needs inequity.

   - Enlighten managers on the opportunity to close non-obvious need gaps.

- Emphasize that staff's higher discretionary efforts will improve the department's performance.
- Ensure that manager's meetings include reviews of departmental PIs to optimize work-need satisfaction through leadership/nurturing macro skills.
- The finance department supports performance by calculating departments' PIs and distributing them to department managers. The corporate PI goes to the CEO and CFO.
- DiaplanU (the online university) develops leadership and nurturing macro skills and staffs' professional skills as they progress on assigned tracks. Learning reports enable feedback and reinforcement.

2. *Accountability:* The chain of command, and its managers at every level, take ownership for embedding and sustaining work needs-equity. Available tools support their responsibility:

- Antecedents and consequences incentivize work-need satisfaction.
- Needs-equity policy is a strong antecedent.
- Performance standards—for example, 80 percent satisfaction levels—provide growth targets for managers.
- Scores on manager's coaching reports spotlight the behaviors of managers that leave specific work needs unsatisfied.
- As higher standards (norms) of care institutionalize, managers' commitment grows. Consecutive impressions of indifference toward staffs' work needs are not in managers' self-interests.

Corrective actions (consequences) include:

- Feedback from one's supervisor.
- Progress reviews on gap-closing strategies.
- Resurveys, progressive actions focusing on developing and reconditioning specific behaviors that resist change.
- Intensified follow-up if resurveys show similar gaps to past surveys.

- Managers conduct recurring meetings on productivity versus need satisfaction, with individual feedback.
- Dismissals should be far down the road. No one tries to fail. The system aids success.

Reinforcement actions (consequences) include:

- Positive feedback on efforts and results.
- Rewards for continually improving survey scores.
- Rewards for attaining extra-mile standing (80 percent satisfaction or higher).
- Rewards for declining productivity indexes.
- Commendations for the changed feelings and attitudes of staff, which raise discretionary effort (engagement).
- Other positive consequences include lower staff turnover and the impact of need satisfaction on other KPIs. Reward as appropriate.

3. *Behavioral Development:*

All of us will change our behaviors when it is in our self-interests. It begins by needing to adapt to (mirror/reflect) our supervisors' behaviors. As environments, norms, and standards change, we adapt to increase our chances of success. We have observed this in multiyear studies. As senior managers increase the intensity and frequency of leadership and nurturing behaviors, a modified group norm (value) develops. Self-interest drives adaptation downline.

Chart D (from a client's research report) is the CEO who supervises the sales director. Chart E is the sales director who supervises the sales managers, whose results are shown in Chart F. Note how behavioral changes in the boss drive behavioral changes downline in direct reports:

Chart D: CEO   Chart E: Sales Director

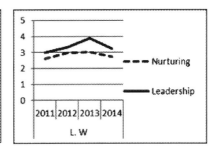

Chart F: Sales Managers

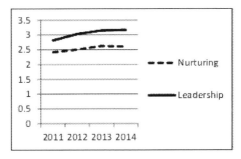

Nurturing: The CEO's nurturing frequency initially trended up, then declined, then plateaued. The sales director's trended up and then declined. Time-lag predicts that nurturing will plateau. Sales managers' nurturing frequency also initially rises, then also plateaus. But it remains at a higher level than at the outset.

Leadership: Leadership's frequency exceeds nurturing's. Therefore, it contributes more highly to total need-satisfaction scores. The Smart16 Survey contains equal nurturing and leadership statements. Equal frequency would yield overlapping graph lines. Given the changes managers were charged with in 2011, goal-oriented behaviors were strongly in demand. The firm changed its marketing and sales business model. However, when objectives were being met by 2013, the frequency of directive behavior declined but remained at a higher level than at inception. In response, sales managers' leadership frequencies rose and then plateaued at a higher level than in 2011. The sales force provided the metrics for sales managers. After their original dip in sales revenues in 2012, sales revenues rose 24 percent by 2014. Leadership frequency mattered. (See chapter 9 referencing this same client's lower PIs and higher sales metrics.)

Regarding survey responses, when staff responds by clicking "Often" or "Always" in unison to a negative survey statement, the boss has a bad ingrained habit. After the survey, he or she is aware of the habit. Others know about it, which puts them and their habit in the spotlight. The needs-equity policy no longer permits frequent denial of a legitimate staff work need. The pinch of *behavioral accountability* is felt. Counterproductive natural behaviors no longer slip silently through the cracks. They make noise.

These external influences raise the frequency of nurturing and leadership behaviors. While managers may not altruistically care about staff needs *yet*, they do care to avert a self-absorbed persona. As they adapt to changed normative values, positive responses from staff reinforce the manager's emerging behaviors. Managers soon perceive that caring serves their self-interests better than not caring. At this point, an in-house university that develops leadership and nurturing competencies is a welcome benefit. As one manager wrote:

> *I am always missing some of my staff's needs. Maybe I could satisfy some more often if I focused on it. There's another survey coming up. It won't look good if my numbers haven't changed and my staff is still sounding off. The productivity index number for my department, I'm worried about it. Sharon told me her ratio is lower than mine, and she hasn't been through management training. But I admit, she's better at caring for her people than I am.*

Being aware, being accountable and being developed foster changes *within* managers.

13

TANGIBLES FROM INTANGIBLES

*When I am working on a problem, I never think
about beauty but when I have finished, if the
solution is not beautiful, I know it is wrong.*

— R. BUCKMINSTER FULLER

THE SOLUTIONS GURUS OFFERED FOR un-engagement haven't been that beautiful, statistically. Anecdotal evidence on management seminars is generally glowing. *Spray and pray* is alive and well in many organizations. But the problem is still staring at us: Managers haven't changed.

Managers have not had strong enough reasons to take better care of their staff needs—until now. We made a start on that in chapter 12 by putting antecedents and consequences in place:

1. Establish work needs-equity between managers and staff.

2. Measure gaps in satisfaction. Make the chain of command aware that gaps erode performance and profit from their departments.

3. Establish accountability for satisfaction of work needs. Reward attainment.

Without an enforced policy, behaviors revert to the mean, which spawns un-engagement. Policy must incarnate in managers' behaviors and performance.

To use an example most people are familiar with from Hollywood, Moses brought down the Ten Commandments from Mount Sinai as policy for the Israelite nation. It didn't cure ills, but it clarified the expected standards for behavior. But as Moses might attest, people *must want* to maintain the standard. External motivation wasn't enough then; it never has been. Violations (like today) emerge regardless of prohibitions.

The Employee Experience

As history has so cruelly demonstrated, not everyone who ends up in power is a great person. Right now, we have a mix. Some great people are in positions of leadership: kind coaches, bosses who empower, politicians who genuinely try to make life a little bit better for others. But many, many authority figures are nothing like that. They lie and cheat and steal, serving themselves while they exploit and abuse others. They are, in a word, corruptible. And they do a lot of damage. (Brian Klaas, *Corruptible: Who Gets Power and How It Changes Us*)

The antecedents and consequences above begin to institutionalize caring. Voluntarily caring is much less common than not caring. Uncaring managers are stuck on the first mile. Yet most really care about their kids. They have an investment there and a paternal or maternal instinct to protect it.

Factoid: Managers are able to care for non-kin. Willingness requires a reason.

So, what makes managers willing to satisfy their staffs' needs? As seen, initially the motivation is extrinsic. Its root is economic security, a survival motivator. Managers are employed to execute needs-equity policies that drive productivity and profit. It is in the firm's mission statement and in managers' job descriptions. A manager may be apathetic and *know it*, but he or she doesn't want to appear apathetic. These extrinsic factors motivate willingness to adapt for social reasons. Why should one care about one's staff? It serves the firm's strategic interests, which one has been hired to serve. It helps one keep one's job and pay one's bills. The solution is not beautiful yet, but we will get there.

Managed care is what hospitals, nursing homes, and assisted-living facilities offer. The quality of that care is the selling point. It is crucial for these businesses' survival. Losing patients is not a good thing in hospitals, especially when it was preventable. The same with nursing homes. Assisted living facilities don't want residents moving out to find better-managed care. Job descriptions in these firms are more explicit. There are personal, legal, and financial extrinsic motivators for caring. Otherwise, their managers and staffs may not voluntarily do so.

Now is the time to insist, *'Why don't we manage how our managers care for their staff?'* (Like humans don't need that!) Will the Reader quibble with this— *we don't care enough*? For legal and oversight reasons, we restrain sexual harassment, overt racial bias, verbal abuse and other maltreatments. We are extrinsically motivated to prevent such. But we don't go further on the Smart16. Going further underpins productivity and profit from our departments.

So, when *acquisition* is taken care of for staff (extrinsic) we flip the management behavioral coin over to intrinsic. This side is *inspiration*. Inspired staff flourish. Managers want to succeed, but without able and willing staff, they won't. Staff wants to succeed. Managers have that going for them. Inspiration provides opportunities for creativity, innovation and recognition for one's prowess. It's engagement's energizer and driver. So … what turns you on in your work as a manager? Is it not something you are good at and enjoy doing? What is the gift or skill that makes you shine at work, that engages you and increases your output? Ok, that is what you are looking for, for your managers and your staff.

- Does their position offer frequent enough opportunities to shine before their peers and you?
- Do they know how important their work and their goals are to the firm?
- Do you tailor projects to their strengths and interests and assign them for personal development?
- Do the assignments provide stretch, pull and challenge?
- Do you build in a fitting reward for completing the project to a high standard?

There is nothing *extrinsic* listed here. These are inspiration triggers - *gap-closing strategies*. Turn these questions into ones you will ask each staff member. (Example: How can I tailor a project to your strengths and interests?) The boss's caring and enthusiasm for each staff member's potential, changes the performance dynamic dramatically. Team success gets into the mix. Under needs-equity, bosses will do for their staff what their supervisors are doing for them. Good will cascades just like ill will.

In chapter 2's table, only three intrinsic needs are listed. Two address *autonomy*—flextime and work-from-home option. *Promote from within* addresses advancement. Let's exceed what's *easy*. Let's do what's *right* for staff and the firm. Let's make people happier and make more profit through opportunities afforded to satisfy every intrinsic motivator.

Suffice it to say, few can flourish in their current positions if they can't exploit the gifts that make them special. *Placement* is crucial for intrinsic satisfaction. Round pegs, round holes. Children practice matching with a wooden or plastic toy. Pros practice it with sophisticated instruments—for example, Predictive Index™, Myers Briggs™, DISC™. Incidentally, these instruments give insight into empathy and altruism relative to behavioral profiles. These virtues come easier for some managers than others. But the altruistic gene is in us. Conditioning that squelches it requires strong behavioral modifiers to override self-interest and surface altruism. Two to three sigma survey gaps (with requirements to close them) is a level of accountability most managers haven't yet felt. That's an unnerving eye-opener and very disruptive to bad interpersonal habits.

Factoid: Good disruptions bring dysfunctions to the surface for treatment.

The extra mile also distinguishes professionals from amateurs. Some amateurs exude toxic apathy. They don't care about their staffs' potential, which breeds inequity, conflict, and fallouts of various sorts. Professionals exude empathy. They practice managed care, which rids the environment of toxic behavior and replaces it with empathy—a breath of fresh air. In the following flow chart, the first box, top right, is the intangible. The last box, bottom left, is the tangible.

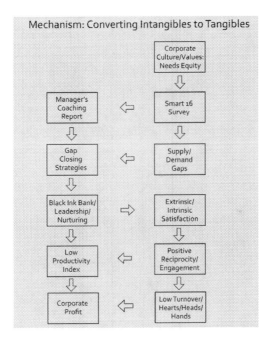

This chain of inputs creates the bottom line. It's managed care for bodies, psyches and finances. It's a *beautiful solution.* Other beautiful things accompany need/desire satisfaction:

The Employee Experience

In a nutshell, happy employees are more productive employees, and more productive employees can seriously boost a company's bottom line.

Anne M. Mulcahy, the former CEO of Xerox, put it a slightly different way when she said, *"Employees who believe that management is concerned about them as a whole person—not just an employee—are more productive, more satisfied, more fulfilled. Satisfied employees mean satisfied customers, which leads to profitability."*

The research backs up Mulcahy in a big way. In its *State of the American Workplace* report, Gallup compared businesses that ranked in the bottom quartile for employee engagement with the businesses in the top quartile when ranked by employee engagement. The report found that the more engaged businesses showed:

-   41 percent less absenteeism, 70 percent fewer safety incidents
-   24 to 59 percent less turnover, 28 percent less shrinkage
-   17 percent greater productivity, 21 percent higher profitability

Increasing your employee engagement can dramatically improve the functioning of your entire office, save you on big costs, reduce turnover, and increase your profits. So how do you do it? Thoey Bou, people operations manager at Poll Everywhere, says, *"People operations is both an art and a science. A lot of companies don't get employee feedback because they don't ask for it … You have to remember that it's a relationship between your business and your people, and that you all have the same goal."* (https://blog.polleverywhere.com/companies-that-excel-employee-engagement/)

14

MACRO-SKILLS TESTED

Men and nations behave wisely once they
have exhausted all the other alternatives.

— A B B A E B A N

Rᴇᴀᴅᴇʀs ᴍᴀʏ ᴛʜɪɴᴋ ᴛʜᴀᴛ ᴅɪꜰꜰᴇʀᴇɴᴛɪᴀᴛɪɴɢ between extrinsic
and intrinsic needs is straightforward, as though one would apply a
nurturing or leadership strategy as a matter of course once a need type
presents. Workshop participants in research partner firms can't usually
select five correct answers when the five situations below are posed
for resolution. One's predisposition to nurture hampers satisfaction of
intrinsic needs. One's instinct to lead may kick in when an extrinsic
need presents. Differentiation is mastered with necessity and practice.
As are all behavioral skills.

> *Factoid: Red ink in the pipeline is automatic if managers*
> *nurture when they should lead, or lead when they should*
> *nurture. Not differentiating is endemic. It's costly because*
> *staff does not respond productively to the wrong stimulus.*

Instincts (hip-shots/knee-jerks) let us down. Staffs' needs suffer. In
the situations posed below, the reader selects, given the need type, one
of four strategies by differentiating between weaker strategies and the

strongest strategy. Respond based on the information provided. The correct response will be a leadership or nurturing strategy, as there are only two categories of needs.

This chapter is longer to cover the five scenarios. Note that managers should lead or nurture in the normal processes of work. It's not *extra work*. The extra mile is the *right work*. Please select the best strategy for resolving each issue.

1. A company is experiencing a loss of regular customers. Over the last few months, the number of customer service complaints has been steadily rising. The sales manager, Alberto Torres, is also responsible for the customer service unit, which is supervised by Sarah Williams. Sarah has been complaining to Alberto about being short-staffed and under stress. Alberto heard from another supervisor that Sarah is thinking about giving her notice. If you were Alberto, would you …

    A. Study the complaints to see which associates receive the most and let Sarah replace them?
    B. Determine if service staff need training, if service standards must be raised, or both, and then make staffing decisions?
    C. Tell Sarah, "Revenues are declining right now; you must improve with the people you have?"
    D. Express empathy for Sarah's situation and authorize additions to the payroll?

    This need is intrinsic. Why? The company's mission is at risk, which makes this scenario about goals, direction, and strategy. Those are leadership issues. Acquiring and retaining customers contributes to the company's mission and purpose. Training can be an extrinsic need, but in this case training is more about mission attainment.

    The correct answer is B. If staff is untrained or service standards are too low or not being met, that is a call for leadership to get out of that situation and back on track to fulfill the mission.

Answer A ignores the training factor. Staff may not need to be replaced. It also ignores the possibility that standards of performance for customer service may not have been set or enforced.

Answer C assumes that improvement is possible without further guidance or support from the managers. Effort alone does not solve all problems.

Answer D raises costs without substantiating the need for it. Some nurturing may be useful, but leadership is what satisfies this intrinsic need.

2. An organization was recently acquired by a larger firm and is undergoing rapid change. Salary and hiring freezes are in place; overtime pay is canceled. Yet workloads are growing, and new demands surface every week.

You manage three copy centers in the company. Your staff is overwhelmed with the volume of work. Quality has suffered. You are getting scathing emails from various department managers. Your staff from the three centers got together. They want a meeting with you. The best strategy for this meeting is to:

A. Apologize for the hiring freeze, overtime restriction, and work volume. Say, "I wish I could make things easier for you, but it's out of my hands until management lifts the restrictions."
B. Let everyone air their grievances. Express appreciation for their efforts. Serve pizza and soft drinks.
C. Review the situation and then ask each staff member how he or she thinks things can be improved.
D. Work at each center two-and-one-half hours per day to catch up on the backlog and meet demand until things settle down or until you can recruit a few more staff.

The correct answer is D. This is an extrinsic need. It calls for support and nurturing. Working conditions are negatively impacting staff. It is not about rewarding and challenging work (intrinsic factors).

It is about the pain the staff is feeling from the workload (extrinsic factor). They need immediate relief. It's time for the boss to roll up his or her sleeves.

Answer A is meaningless nurturing. It's more of a cop-out. It isn't constructive and leaves staff in the same miserable situation.

Answer B can bring some temporary relief but will not improve day-to-day conditions. Again, it is nurturing without resolution.

Answer C brings out staff input. That's an aspect of leadership, but without full-blown brainstorming with outside experts or senior management's participation, it probably won't produce a solution that gets around the policy. Even if the manager takes the matter high up the chain of command, it could take weeks to get approval for additional staff. They need relief now, or they will begin resigning.

> *Factoid: Nurturing never appears in definitions of management. Definitions reflect firms' needs, not staffs' needs.*

3. Michael was hired six months ago. He has performed well to this point. But Anne, his supervisor, has recently noticed what she thinks is a loss of interest or motivation in his job. Last week he extended his lunch break by fifteen minutes to finish a crossword puzzle. Yesterday, as she turned the corner past his workstation, she spotted a job board on his browser before he closed it. She doesn't want to lose Mike, but one of his coworkers told Anne that Mike seemed bored and distracted, and she thinks his work standards are declining.

The appropriate action for Anne to take in this situation is to:

A. Confront Mike over things she has noticed and the comment a colleague (anonymously) made about him.
B. Have a discussion with Mike about his work and motivation. Get to the root of his issue and then build motivators into his job.

C. Assure Mike of her support and ask for his commitment to maintaining a high standard of performance.
D. Delegate some of her work to Mike to keep him busy and challenged.

The correct answer is B. Until Anne discovers the real issue affecting Mike's change in performance, she can't take appropriate action to retain him and keep him performing well. This issue needs Anne's leadership as it is an intrinsic motivator. Mike is now unengaged. The likely reason is that the job no longer challenges him or sustains his interest. That can easily occur within the first six months in lower-level jobs.

Job enrichment is the best strategy. It includes the following:

- Higher level work
- More difficult work
- Work that brings out one's best skills
- Work that grows one's competencies
- Work that prepares one for advancement

Answer A comes on too strongly, as if Mike is guilty. Everyone has extended their lunch break at some point. So far, this was a one-time event. Looking for another job says as much about the company as it does about Mike. People often leave for reasons that employers overlook.

Answer C is asking Mike for improved performance without delving into the reason for his performance decline.

Answer D could be a positive leadership move. But keeping Mike busy is not a long-term solution. Not if the work is not challenging and isn't real job enrichment. If it isn't, Mike won't stay.

4. A manufacturing firm added many employee benefits over several decades. Benefits are competitive with those offered by other firms in the same industry. Yet associates' turnover continued at 30 percent annually, at least double the acceptable (10 to 15 percent) level.

Which of the following strategies would be most advisable for executive management to take to significantly reduce turnover?

A. Add additional benefits that competitors are not offering, like subsidized cafeteria meals.
B. Pay managers an additional bonus if they can get their departments' turnover rates under 20 percent.
C. Survey satisfaction of work needs frequently. Close need gaps with targeted strategies.
D. Pay employees a significant bonus for each completed year of employment.

The correct answer is C. Topping the list of staff work needs are opportunities to satisfy intrinsic motivators in the course of their work. The manager leads staff to a place of psychological well-being. Failure to do so degrades the relationship and is one of the main reasons staff resigns.

Answer A raises costs. An extrinsic satisfier will never offset an unsatisfied intrinsic motivator, though it may help a staff member to gravitate to intrinsic satisfiers.

Answer B raises costs. Managers should not have to be paid twice when it is already their job to retain staff by satisfying their work needs.

Answer D also raises costs. Employees who are happy in their work—both types of needs are satisfied—do not have to be paid bonuses to stay.

5. An ambitious VP of Sales is eager to exceed the goal he attained last year, which was a company record. To succeed, his team must generate 15 percent more revenue this year. Three factors work against him and his team: (1) A new product launch, which was supposed to account for 30 percent of revenues, was delayed until the beginning of the second quarter; (2) A new competitor entered the market with a similar product; (3) There is a moderate downturn

in the economy due to high interest rates. Account executives (AEs) and customer service representatives (CSRs) feel pressured, untrained, and stretched to the limit. They get a big bonus if they reach the VP's goal but are quite doubtful that it's realistic. When they share their concerns, the VP brushes it off as "nerves we have to fight off." By the end of the second quarter, over 20 percent of the AEs have resigned. CSRs were forced into AE jobs without training. Six dropped out last month.

Which of the following strategies would you advise the VP of Sales to implement?

A. Stick to your goals. People thrive best on a challenge and the prospect of breaking records.
B. Identify the "whiners," and replace them with highly ambitious closers.
C. Revise the goal to match last year's performance. Train after hours on overtime pay. Let CSRs take over AE's admin work.
D. Raise the sales commission rate on all sales by 5 percent. Discount the new product by 10 percent.

The best answer is C. These are nurturing actions to address extrinsic needs. Going too far or too fast for people can leave them behind. They resign, as some have. Attaining the same goal as last year is a superior goal if attained under more difficult circumstances. Overtime pay for training is a win-win for the VP, the AEs, and the CSRs. Asking CSRs to do AEs' admin work, but still qualify for the bonus if AEs hit the goal, is fair. When things are ready to explode, take the pressure off. Nurture to keep them in the game.

Answer A is very high risk. Capacity has been reached under the circumstances. A high bar with a low chance of scaling it makes too many people walk away.

Answer B discounts people's feelings. It will be an unpopular decision to fire these people. Those who stay will be fearful of sharing their genuine concerns.

Answer D raises costs and reduces revenues. Incentives can only work when there is spare capacity. This team is at capacity now.

Leadership concerns objectives, goals, direction, and strategy. Direction and strategy include moving to a better psychological place through job enrichment. Hungry psyches is about intrinsic satisfaction (more on that in chapter 19). Nurturing concerns satisfying basic necessities— like belonging, tools, training and good working conditions. It's also about comforting, encouraging, and relieving stress. But strong caution is necessary:

> Managers who are natural nurturers will bring that behavior to every situation. Many situations call for direction, goals, challenges and opportunities for achievement. Even though staff may be experiencing some discomfort, pampering is not what they need in this case. Complaining stops when staff gets enthusiastic about accomplishing something significant. They need inspiration, not acquisition. They need leadership macro skills. It's about where the department is going, that will take staff to a better place? Sell it. Lead the way. Reward attainment.

The manager's coaching report (next chapter) offers nurturing and leadership strategies when and where each is required. The two are always differentiated. When both are required, strategies target them separately. These macro skills are relevant in society at large. We are wiser if we also differentiate them— by short or long-term benefit.

Extrinsic benefits bring short-term relief for constituents experiencing economic hardship. This is often necessary. But lifting people to a higher economic plane means opportunity and challenge— intrinsic motivators. These don't break the bank— they close economic gaps. Productivity is our long-term saving grace.

Let's recap with a relational, outcome-based definition of *management:*

Management is the act of institutionalizing needs-equity by applying two macro skills—leadership and nurturing— in sufficient intensity/frequency to satisfy all associates' 16 work needs. Satisfaction, especially of intrinsic needs, fuels workforce engagement and productivity, lowers payroll costs relative to revenues, and raises profits.

This definition is the bedrock for business goals and organizational development. In the next chapter, we discuss action plans to close need gaps measured in the Smart16 Survey. Positive reciprocity is an earned response.

15

RUBBER MEETS ROAD

*Have a bias towards action—let's see something
happen now. You can break that big plan into
small steps and take the first step right away.*

—INDIRA GANDHI

THIS CHAPTER IS ABOUT CLOSING need gaps. It's tempting for the
reader to gloss over it. But that's what created the brutal employee
experience on the last page of this chapter. Please think it through. The
rubber meets the road right here.

If PIs are not declining, needs-equity policies are not being applied. This
chapter sets out small, crucial steps to institutionalize needs-equity. It
brings the biggest payoff possible.

A manager may have several two to three sigma gaps across the 16
needs. While each must be closed, action plans should be limited to two
statements after each survey. Narrow focus prevents dilution of effort.
Accountability is established up front, but compliance is incremental.
Behavioral development requires ample practice-feedback, at a controlled
pace, to satisfy the spectrum of work needs.

All senior managers conduct one-on-one meetings with their managers who have two or more direct reports. Senior managers' input on budget, policy, timing, authority and the big picture is essential. Senior managers also improve their own survey analytics when the staffs of their direct reports are more productive.

The plan is short-term, for the interim before the next survey. The intended outcome is for managers to execute coaching report strategies by tailoring them individually to close work needs gaps. Schedule time for these meetings.

One-on-One Meeting Agenda

1. Overall Review of the Survey:

   In the face-to-face (or virtual) meeting, the senior manager and his or her direct report review the direct report's complete manager's coaching report. This is accessed on the online platform. A video explains its use. This review covers every section of the report in preparation for detailed feedback to follow.

2. Feedback Discussion:

   The senior manager provides feedback on the manager's performance on need satisfaction. He or she:

   - Leads a discussion on sigma gaps from staff's responses to survey statements. Three sigma gaps are reviewed first, then two sigma gaps, then one sigma.

   - Asks the manager for his or her input on why the gaps exist; responds to the manager's answers by leading and/or nurturing the manager in closing gaps

   - Compares the previous two surveys' metrics with the current survey's metrics.

- If scores haven't improved on specific statements, asks for reasons why leadership and nurturing behaviors have been impeded; determines if further action is necessary.

- If scores have improved, recognizes the manager for leading or nurturing more strongly and more often.

- Senior manager notes the satisfaction percentage on the last page of the manager's coaching report. Scores under 80 percent generally indicate unengaged staff and first-mile managers; cautions managers that low satisfaction scores account for lower productivity and higher labor costs than necessary. This affects his or her department's contribution to profits.

- Senior manager advises that, initially, extrinsic scores may be higher than intrinsic scores. Asks manager to increase focus on intrinsic needs. This includes generating possibilities for enriching each staff member's job scope, depth, and growth opportunities.

While the senior manager is reviewing the complete report, he or she advises the manager that comprehensive improvement in all 16 work needs is not expected before the next survey. All gaps will be addressed over the long term, approximately three years. However, behavioral development before the next survey focuses on two statements. Senior managers exhibit high expectations for closing the gaps in focus.

3. Selecting Gaps to Focus on:

- In developing action plans, the senior manager selects two statements with the biggest variances.

- The gaps would likely be two or three sigma variances from the norm—the manager's weakest performances on work-need satisfaction.

- Such gaps inhibit engagement and productivity. The solution is increased intensity and frequency of nurturing and/or leadership—the manager's focus for short-term action plans.

4. Behavioral Development Strategies:

The senior manager and direct report discuss the strategies provided in the manager's coaching report. The senior manager asks:

- How will each strategy address the gap?

- Of the two to four strategies the coaching report offers for each unmet work need, which is likely to be most effective at this time in his or her work unit? (Staff input covered next, is crucial.)

- The senior manager, with his or her direct report, sets limits on solutions the direct report can implement with his or her associates. Among the limitations for consideration are budgets, operational constraints and company policies.

- He or she shows that gaps don't close without behavioral development, and development does not occur without an assessed need for learning, a requirement to learn, effective learning tools, and learning metrics.

DiaplanU provides a behavioral learning foundation. It develops the competencies that satisfy extrinsic and intrinsic needs.

- The senior manager reviews learning progress from the learning management system (LMS) reports and raises any pertinent learning issues with the manager.

Factoid: There are only two ways a manager can impact an employee's output: motivation and training. If you are not training, you are neglecting half the job. Andy Grove

Following the meeting with his or her boss, the manager returns to review survey results with his or her team, in person or virtually. There are two items on this meeting's agenda:

1. The manager thanks team members for their candid feedback and for sharing how strongly and how often they have feelings about unmet work needs. The manager explains how staff responses to statements support his or her development and are critical for department and company goals.

2. The manager shares the two survey statements under review. Then he or she:

   - Discusses statement(s) with staff; the key is to obtain strong input from staff.

   - Brainstorms the causes of unsatisfied needs and possible solutions.

   - Records ideas on a flipchart/whiteboard, and asks, "What problems are being caused by unmet work needs? How do they affect everyone's performance?" The manager records staff's responses.

   - Conducts a discussion on which strategies from the brainstorming are most feasible and will be the strongest contributors to work-need satisfaction.

   - Summarizes the agreed-on strategy(s) or action plans listed on the flipchart or whiteboard. Smartphone pictures can preserve data.

   Factoid: When people are financially invested, they want a return. When people are emotionally invested, they want to contribute.　　　　　　　　　　　　　　Simon Sinek

- Combines staff input with his or her inputs and his or her senior manager's inputs to arrive at a mutually agreed action plan to satisfy the work needs,

- Assures staff that they and you, their manager, have the senior manager's support and guidance while implementing chosen solutions.

- Sends a summary email to the senior manager and to staff on the final action plan.

At this point, the staff knows they were heard, and management has responded by taking action to meet their work needs. The manager should also invite the staff to discuss any other pressing need affecting performance. Awareness and transparency are invaluable to collaboration.

The gaps in focus begin shrinking across the organization because all managers took a few small action steps on the extra mile. Managers understand their roles in motivation. Positive reciprocity increases. The employee experience improves. The next survey's scores improve. The need satisfaction bell curve shifts to the right.

My Employee Experience

At age seventeen, I found a good-paying job as a laborer for a roofing company, still in business in Denver today. The firm had the contract for a new roof on South High School. The clay tiles were in four boxcars on a rail siding near Alameda Avenue. My boss and I drove there in a ten-ton flatbed. A similar company truck was already parked there. We backed up to the first boxcar, opened it, and started carrying out tiles. It was August. By late morning, the temperature was in the high 80s. Each tile weighed ten pounds. My boss and I each carried six at a time.

Within a half hour, my T-shirt was soaked with sweat. I took it off to cool down. Loose grit from the tile edges started collecting around my beltline. Within an hour, my waist was raw and burning from abrasions and salt. By the time the flatbeds were loaded, I wasn't fit to continue. But we had to get the tiles to South High. There, sadly, the trucks (I drove the second one) couldn't get over the curb and up to the school buildings. Which is where wheelbarrows came in handy.

We each hauled up twenty-four tiles per wheelbarrow load. There was a bank to climb before getting up to flatter turf. No way could a wheelbarrow be pushed up it. We backed up the bank dragging them. By then, the jagged edges of the tiles had eaten through my gloves. Exposed fingers grew blisters from the wheelbarrow handles. When they popped, the grit was brutal. Impairments severely hampered my productivity.

The guys on the roof kept hollering for more tiles. It took 150,000 over several days to cover two acres of buildings. We couldn't cope. Three laborers arrived from another jobsite to help. Over those days, I loaded, unloaded, and wheelbarrowed about 25,000 tiles at ten pounds each (+-125 tons). I didn't complain; I needed the work. I thought I wasn't man enough for the job.

Coveralls or thick aprons and a supply of leather gloves, if provided by the company, would have saved my hands and midriff. I know now that is simple first-mile management. A cooler full of water, or preferably sodas, would have cooled us off and replenished calories. My boss had hung a canvas water bag from the truck's side mirror. The water was warm, but it kept us functioning.

These painful memories sensitized me. At a minimum, extrinsic needs must be met. Upward mobility (intrinsic) must include the front line, often disproportionately served by racial minorities. The fondest hope at the lowest rung is to enjoy what seems out of reach. Caring organizations will optimize everyone's potential to accrue more benefits through personal and professional growth. We will not know anyone's potential until we give them the chance to exploit it. Raw gifts are all around us, waiting to be utilized. Waiting to add more value to our enterprises.

16

MANAGERS WILL LEARN: WHY AND HOW

There are two primary choices in life: to accept conditions as they exist, or accept the responsibility for changing them.

—DENNIS WAITLEY

WHY WOULD A MANAGER AVOID doing online training to be a better manager? Because it is easier to behave as one chooses and hope that others won't notice one's unengaged/disengaged staff.

Why would a manager do online training to become a better manager? Because the Smart16 Survey shows the result of behaving as one chooses:

1. Staff's work needs do not get satisfied.
2. Staff negatively reciprocates toward their manager for ignoring their needs.
3. Negative reciprocity erodes staff productivity.
4. More staff is needed to get the work done.
5. More staff raises payroll costs.
6. Higher payroll costs erode profits.
7. The manager is not fully doing the job he or she is paid to do.

The Employee Experience

I had a boss and she had to be the laziest person I've ever worked with. We worked in a section of the grocery store (deli) that was by far the busiest one in the store. It was chronically short-staffed. She would work a maximum of two hours per day on her shift. Every other manager worked virtually the whole day to make it work.

The rest of the day she would go up to her office eating donuts and playing Candy Crush (back when that was popular). She might occasionally stroll down to bark out some more orders. I lasted like three months but in that time like 15-20 people got hired and quit, most on the exact day they were hired because of her.

Nasty, rude, mean, trashy and felt like being the manager made her queen of the castle. It didn't. I learned that about three months after I left, she did get fired. Because literally every single person left in order to find work elsewhere.

Source: https//forum.mrmoneynustache.com/welcome-to-the-forum'experiences-working-for-a-bad-boss/

Of course, this boss was in serious need of leadership and nurturing training. Managers are hired to generate profit by building and maintaining productive teams. If that purpose is not supported to a firm's satisfaction, it's reasonable—and impelling—to take action to attain its purpose: *needs–equity for attaining healthy ROI for owners/investors.*

As productivity is rooted in managers' behaviors with their staffs, behavioral development becomes a priority. Nowadays, e-learning is the least costly learning medium. So, on what grounds may managers decline to participate? The next question: How effective is online behavioral development? The answer: To the degree its results correlate with declining departmental productivity indices.

Finally, what does online behavioral learning look like when results correlate with declining productivity indices?

> *Factoid: To change any behavior we have to slow down and act intentionally rather than from habit and impulse. (Henna Inam)*

We established that intense, frequent leadership and nurturing macro skills satisfy the staff's 16 work needs to the extra-mile level. But that takes time. Cause-effect technology controls the rising curve of need satisfaction. The instruments are:

1. *Pretests.* Learners document current frequency of use (seldom, sometimes, often, always) of the competency in focus. Objective statements assess current knowledge.

2. *Small-Dose Learning Units (approximately six minutes).* Ample behavioral practice facilitates adult behavioral learning. Unit exercises are downloaded for application with one's staff, or with one's own tasks.

3. *Animated Videos.* Text, graphics, narration, and background music engage learners through sensory appeal and continuous interaction. Approximately fifteen units per module offer frequent job applications to real-time situations. Learners may advance after completing required practice rounds.

4. *Post-tests.* Learners document increased frequency of use of new competencies. Reports compare post-test scores to pretests to assess cognitive/behavioral development.

5. *Thirty-five Modules.* These are divided into 500 learning units. These provide a comprehensive, small-dosed, competency-based curriculum for managers' and staffs' professional development. Learning tracks are assigned based on levels of job responsibilities.

Assessment and development leverage institutionalizing. Future Smart16 surveys capture increased frequency and strength of competencies and rising need satisfaction. Periodic measurements, with feedback and continuing education, prevent regression.

17

GRABBING THE REINS

*Leaders inspire accountability through their ability
to accept responsibility before they place blame.*

— COURTNEY LYNCH

Pointed Questions: Do They Apply?

1. As a CEO, how would it affect you if you learned that two-thirds of your associates commiserate with family on how little your managers care about their work needs?
2. What would be your level of concern for corporate profit if it's forfeited because two-thirds of your managers fail to care for their staffs' work needs?
3. What concern would you have about the ROI/dividends investors forfeit if your firm is failing to satisfy many of your people's work needs?
4. If you felt responsibility for such outcomes (given an effective alternative was available), would you act to make your staff, firm, and shareholders better off?

SHOULD THESE FOUR POINTS APPLY and you intend to address them, you will need help from a licensed, certified consulting firm to implement this system and all tools. Transformations often fail, but when installed and monitored, as set out here, you will succeed. Consultants guide firms in navigating steps 1-10 below. (See contact information in the "Afterword" for consulting support.)

For Action: As Applicable

1. *Announce Needs-Equity Policy:* Send a detailed, personalized email to all managers and staff. A sample letter is included here.
2. *Implement Needs-Equity Policy:* Include needs-equity policy in your mission statement, your employee handbook, and your orientation and onboarding programs.
3. *Add the Smart16 table to Managers' Job Descriptions:* Include requirements to satisfy them.
4. *Rework Your KPIs to Place High Priority on Staff's Work-Need Satisfaction:* Need satisfaction, in tandem with department PI scores, should account for 25 percent of the total on scheduled performance evaluations.
5. *Administer the Smart16 Survey Three times annually:* Following each, build short-term action plans to close needs gaps. For the sharpest analytics, at least 90 percent of staff must complete it. It takes only twelve minutes on smartphones and laptops.
6. *Assign Management Development Tracks (chapter 12) to Grow Leadership-Nurturing Skills that Close Gaps:* Assign tracks to staff for professional skills, career-development, and life goals.
7. *Structure Bonus System:* Offer rewards to managers for rising need-satisfaction and falling departmental and corporate PIs.
8. *Publicly Recognize Extra-Mile Managers:* Set a need satisfaction goal of 80 percent or above.
9. *Return a Fair Percentage of Increased Profits:* Reward staff and managers who helped you and the company reach established goals. Rewarded behavior is behavior repeated.
10. *Free Apathetic Managers:* Allow managers with persistent needs gaps to seek positions elsewhere.

These steps get firms grounded in the system. But there is ongoing analytical work stemming from corporate reports. Your consultant will be with you for the long term.

If you are an ambitious business person, you can get quite far by answering certain questions:

> *What* do I want to do?
> *Why* do I want to do it?
> *When* do I want to do it?
> *How* will I do it?
> *Where* will I do it?

To go any farther, you may have to ask, "*Who* can help me?" From that point, you will likely become a boss, with your agendas and your staffs' agendas operating in sync—or at odds.

Of course, our agendas take precedence over an associate's agenda. We are the bosses of our investments. Our needs are more important. So, needs become inequitable. Our staff members start asking similar questions:

> *What* do I want from this job?
> *Why* would I take it and keep it long-term?
> *When* will my needs and aspirations get met?
> *Who* will help me be successful here?

That last *who factor* can compete with our agenda. If we give time and effort to our associates' needs, we may be distracted and spend less time and effort on our own missions.

> *Factoid: If we treat our staff as we want to be treated, the Who Factor doesn't distract us, it attracts our staff. They come aboard, stay aboard and row hard.*

> *Factoid:* ♫♪ *I would do anything for love* ♫♪. (Meatloaf, RIP)

Staff decides what's in their best interest, including to stay or resign. When people leave, the firm lost the battle in their minds. People leave bosses who don't appreciate them. Staff with managers who fire up their intrinsic motivators hang in for the long haul. What's the reality for your frontline staff?

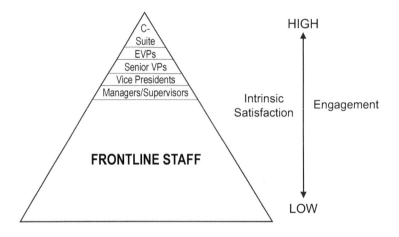

They represent 80% of most organizations. What is your firm's total payroll cost? If that dropped by a conservative 5% of revenues, how much extra profit would be gleaned? That is your Behavioral ROI: How you attain it and sustain it.

18

C-SUITE'S NEW PLAYBOOK

*Smart CFOs embrace technology to shift
the focus of their team from transactions
and reports to strategic thinking*

— CFO.UNIVERSITY

*Factoid: No one has ever run to a finance department to get
treated better.*

(HR Staffer)

C︎AN READERS IMAGINE THE FINANCE department being involved in how associates are treated? We know how managers' handling of staffs' work needs correlates with profit or loss. So, will CFOs keep overlooking the impact of intangibles on year-end financials? If this is not their primary fiduciary responsibility, whose is it? Intangible metrics are not interlopers in the finance department. They rank as highly as gross margin and expense control. A financial controller must control what is controllable if it contributes to profit. It's his or her baby, but this one is currently in the HR foster home.

After introducing needs-equity, three-year profit projections will be up to 100 higher, other factors being normal. Expect the PI to drop five percentage points by the end of the third year. That adds about 5 percent of revenues to profits. A firm netting six percent should net +-11 percent by the end of year three, an 83.33 percent increase. Users find their own sweet spot for how low their PI can go, but much extra profit is there to extract.

Projections based on a new productivity strategy enable managers to revise performance targets. Our outcome examples are reasonable approximations for forecasting. A mantle of ownership, expressed through purpose, discipline, candor and good communications, underpins success. The CEO and CFO own gross margin and expense controls; therefore they own the behavioral ROI from needs-equity that is sitting in their third bucket (PI).

Chief Executive Officer's Role:

1. After working through *The Extra-Mile Manager,* CEOs should assign it to the CFO for reading, discussion, decisions and rollout.
2. The management board must sign on to needs-equity. It isn't caving to demand or placating. It's rational, fair, and in the associates' and firm's best interests.
3. CEOs send personal emails to all staff and managers regarding the needs-equity policy, including its purpose and benefits.
4. CEOs meet with their direct reports. Prepare them to execute the policy and the actions that drive and sustain changes.
5. Having gained control of intangibles, CEO's forecast higher earnings. How will new profits coming into the pipeline be incorporated into strategic plans? What will the new profits be used for—growth, market share, R&D? What portion of increased profits is shared with associates and managers who brought the results?
6. Find a way to involve associates in formulating plans. Try to see them as partners in profit. Their vantage points can modify objectives and increase collaboration and motivation. Work to overcome us-and-them mindsets.

Chief Financial Officer's Role:

1. The CFO is responsible for calculating the benchmark PI. Usually, this is the ratio of payroll to revenues for the last fiscal year. If the last year was an anomaly, the last two or three years can be averaged and used. This final number ($Payroll ÷ $Revenues = PI) must be thoughtfully calculated. It's the baseline against which future PIs are compared. Forecast profit projections based on new controlled sources of profit (the third bucket).

2. The finance department will maintain the PIs for corporate and every department. Department managers display the PI graphs finance sends to them. Awareness (covered earlier) is essential. Visibility maintains it.

3. Schedule three Smart16 surveys per fiscal year:

   - These reveal needs-equity gaps. Bell curves on satisfaction levels will shift right (rising need satisfaction). Concurrently, PI scores should reflect a declining ratio of payroll to revenues.
   - Anomalies should be investigated by chains of command and action plans developed to improve metrics.
   - Reward declining PI trends. Liaise with HR. Recognize best performing departments. How much did their payroll savings contribute to profits?
   - Managers don't compete with other departments, only with themselves to better their last scores.

4. Liaise with department managers to include PIs on meeting agendas. Provide the metrics they need for reviews.

5. Ensure that all finance managers and staff complete all assigned online courses and set examples for all departments in needs-equity and payroll savings.

The Chief HR Officer's role:

1. *Upgrading Managers' Job Descriptions:* HR works with CEOs and CFOs to include needs-equity policy and performance in managers' job descriptions.
2. *Restructuring Managers' Performance Evaluations:* Allocate 25 percent of the final score to Smart16 scores and departmental PIs.
3. *Preparing Database for Smart16 Surveys:* Maintain an accurate database. Liaise with licensed consulting firms to upload the database for scheduled distributions of Smart16 surveys. Excel master is provided.
4. *Planning Logistics:* This should include the two-day managers' certification training on the Smart16 Survey and DiaplanU (The Third Bucket of Profit Workshop).
5. *Maintaining Smart16 Records:* These include scores, online training, issuing learning management systems (LMS) reports, classroom training certificates, and awards for declining PIs.
6. *Issuing Awards and Bonuses for Extra-Mile Manager (80 Percent) Smart16 Survey scores.* As incorporated in policy, share percentages of additional profits earned with all staff. You want repeat performance.
7. *Liaising with C-Suite and Line/Staff Organizations.* Collaborate with operating departments on system deployment and related employee-management matters.

Shared Roles in the C-Suite: Needs-equity is a cultural transformation. It begins as a top-down initiative, but its effect is bottom-up positive reciprocity—engagement. Demonstrating to associates that their needs are as important as management's engenders a new perspective of the firm and management. Management has done it to play fair.

Further, Item 23 on the Smart16 Survey is an open question: *"If the organization, or your immediate boss, could do one thing to make you happier at your job, what would it be?"* We see simple statements, paragraphs and short stories as responses. You want to hear them. Many are complimentary; many raise eyebrows.

People expect action on their inputs. Study responses, list them on your agenda to take action and report back to staff. There are many more associates than managers. Their collective impact, when motivated, is like hiring 20 percent more people who work hard for free.

Lower need satisfaction scores may stem from managers with low emotional intelligence (EQ) scores. Some managers are less sensitive to their people's work needs. Under needs-equity, the pain of staying the same will be greater than the pain of changing. Low scores are a loud call for more intrinsic satisfiers. Managers of low EQs should diplomatically, but unyieldingly, keep the needs-equity standard on the table and require alignment.

High-EQ managers are open to feedback and coaching. Staff responds better to their higher levels of empathy. Associates know their voices are being heard. This, more than any other factor, transforms cultures. You rolled up your sleeves for them. If it didn't feel comfortable or normal, it will as you continue it. Thinking (and the brain) changes as we practice prosocial skills.

You have figured out how a business actually works, *behaviorally*. It's what people need and want. It's motivation! As the C-Suite reorders priorities to better serve their people's needs, if fanfare is avoided and no one solicits commendation for their compassion, they'll be taken seriously. Do it because people need and desire the same things as C-Suite execs. Ask yourself: *Do I always provide leadership and nurturing?* If your staff thinks *Yes,* then they are your greatest asset.

19

POLARITY TO PARTNERSHIP

*The true test of character is to live win-win even when
promoted to positions where win-lose is possible.*

— ORRIN WOODWARD

LET'S GO DEEPER INTO NEEDS-EQUITY. It is a major cultural change
in associates' standing in the organization. The rationale for internal
cultural change is compelling: Associates' work lives are very different
from managers' work lives. The disparity is stark.

Some managers embrace this flawed dichotomy: *Authority is superiority;
subordination is inferiority.* That feeds the us-them mindset. Considering
staffs' capacity to positively impact results is smart. They make up 80
percent of the workforce. If they are firing on half of their cylinders,
it's woefully expensive. As tiny as they are, every ant in a colony, every
bee in a hive, labors for the survival of all. We all have the same 16
work needs; we all equally deserve satisfaction. Staff begins saying,
"us," and, "we" when we level the intrinsic playing field. Their other
cylinders kick in.

Staff's intrinsic satisfaction and engagement levels intertwine. The
disparity in intrinsic satisfaction raises staff turnover, while manager
turnover remains low and static. Recruitment and training costs from

staff turnover dwarf the costs of manager turnover. People stay long term when they grow, when their job is fulfilling. Let's use an analogy:

The leader steers the bike and chooses the destination and route to take. Those behind can't choose any aspect to their satisfaction. Their view is restricted and it never changes. Their efforts may not be noted or recognized.

Extrinsic needs, like refreshments and rest stops, may be overlooked. Intrinsic desires like input on decisions that affect them, achieving a personal best in time or distance, or visiting interesting destinations may not be realized. Are they engaged for the long term? How long will they continue to pedal hard?

These intrinsic satisfiers for managers are not available to entry-level and frontline staff:

Management's Trust	Higher Visibility, Influence Power
Delegated authority with discretionary judgment	Access to privileged information, company plans, power to influence
Autonomy, flexibility in handling tasks	Management bonus status
More variety in job tasks; special assignments	Placement in succession plans
Comradery with senior managers	Seminars and business travel

How can the frontline workforce be more fully engaged now? How can we prepare them for advancement so more satisfiers are theirs to enjoy down the road? Targeted strategies activate Smart16 motivators 9 through 16. Managers using this system can review those in their manager's coaching report and begin applying them. Readers may use these strategies to close intrinsic gaps:

Smart16 Intrinsic Motivators	Hands-On, Gap-Closing Strategies
9. Work that interests and challenges me and uses my best skills.	What tasks bring out an individual's best skills? Are these what individuals like doing most? Are they available in your unit? Mismatches happen when skills aren't assessed in recruitment. The Predictive Index™ matches tasks to work behavior profiles. The Telos Skills Inventory™ assesses a wide range of work skills. Placement elsewhere may be beneficial to both units. If not addressed, Smart16 gaps persist. Ask HR for assistance.
10. Grow my competency, knowledge, skills, and experience through my job.	Cross-training, standing in for the supervisor and special assignments tailored to skills and interests raise motivation and job satisfaction. Train staff to perform increasingly higher-level tasks. Set creative challenges on improving work processes or outcomes. Reward good ideas.
11. Have the autonomy and authority to perform my job as I think best.	Train fully in all job tasks and then delegate responsibility and accountability for results. Make expectations on standards, quantity, and quality clear.
12. Know that my work is contributing to the organization's goals.	Use flow charts to show how their work flows into department results that support the firm's business objectives and customer satisfaction.
13. Receive recognition and rewards for my performance.	Show your appreciation. Use staff meetings to praise staff members before peers. Be specific as to why it matters. Reward proportional to performance. Don't miss chances to give positive feedback. It supports future performance.

14. Relate well with my colleagues and have their respect.	Encourage team spirit (us and we). Use team activities to increase collaboration. Establish team ownership of units' outcomes. In staff meetings, highlight each's contribution individually. Draw out input from reticent staff members. Give everyone a chance in the limelight. Encourage sharing of feelings so no one feels emotionally isolated.
15. Participate in decisions and have my suggestions valued.	Solicit staff's input in decisions that they have some stake or interest in. Recognize contributions. Report back on good results from their inputs. Give public credit.
16. Have the opportunity to advance and achieve my life's purpose.	Know the dreams and ambitions of each staff member. Discuss purpose, life goals, and milestones to attain enroute. Share the company's vision. How do their jobs contribute to the firm's vision and their own vision?

The remainder of this chapter is a sample communication from the CEO to all employees. It is personalized by using each associate's or manager's name. It informs them about the firm's decision to implement a needs-equity policy, the changes related to its implementation, and the benefits accruing to associates and the firm.

The Firm's Letterhead

Dear (Associate's or Manager's name):

Our firm, (Its name), decided to implement a *needs-equity policy*. Inequity in work-need satisfaction is not win-win and it strains relationships between management and staff. Your work needs are as important as your manager's and the firm's needs. If your managers have not met your work needs, they probably didn't know precisely what your work needs are or how best to satisfy them.

Extensive studies over decades have identified 16 universal, crucial work needs comprised of two types: extrinsic and intrinsic. There are eight of each as the table below lists. If each of your motivators was satisfied, consider how it would impact your motivation and job performance:

Extrinsic Motivators: I need to ...	Intrinsic Motivators: I desire to ...
1. Be treated fairly and equally with others.	9. Have interesting and challenging work that utilizes my best skills.
2. Have my group's acceptance.	
3. Have necessary tools, resources, information and instructions to do my job.	10. Grow my competencies, knowledge, skills and experience through my job.
4. Be trusted to do good work.	11. Have the autonomy and authority to perform my job as I think best.
5. Always know what my boss expects from me.	
6. Have a supportive boss who helps solve problems that affect me.	12. Know that my work is contributing to the organization's goals.
7. Have my work unit/department be well organized.	13. Receive recognition and rewards for my performance.
8. Receive good pay and benefits and fair evaluations of my performance.	14. Relate well with my colleagues and have their respect.
	15. Participate in decisions and have my suggestions valued.
	16. Have opportunities to advance and to achieve my life's purpose.

All managers in the firm now have this Smart16 list in their job descriptions. The Smart16 Survey identifies need gaps requiring your manager's attention. While all associates have all 16 needs, how strongly and how often each arises, varies individually. It takes twelve minutes to complete the survey via smartphone, tablet, or computer. The manager's coaching report, derived from the survey, provides strategies that tailor satisfiers to you personally.

Of course, all managers also have all these needs. Their immediate supervisor is responsible for meeting their needs. I, as CEO, am also accountable to meet the work needs of my direct reports. Each chain-of-command will oversee needs satisfaction for all its people.

A key part of the needs-equity system is an online university called DiaplanU. Your manager will be learning skills to guide and support you when and how you need it. The university also has a track for associates. You'll develop professional skills to support your success and your career with the firm.

You have gifts, which is why you were chosen to join us. We commit to your personal and professional development. Your manager will discuss development opportunities with you. These will prepare you for higher challenges and advancement. Every four months, you'll let your manager know how well he or she is doing. You remain anonymous. When your manager reviews results with your team, satisfaction gaps are discussed, and solutions are brainstormed. When your gap(s) is in focus, describe how the gap hinders your performance. When solutions are asked for, submit your proposed solution. You are probably not the only one with a particular need gap.

The needs-equity system improves productivity and profit. As such, it's a *financial* tool, ultimately owned by me and the CFO, with all managers and staff contributing. The firm is more prosperous as we manage the behavioral inputs that create value. Impediments to your performance are removed and replaced with opportunities for job satisfaction.

The founders of (firm's name) had a dream. As that dream materialized, your talents became necessary to take the firm further. You have a dream. We want to know about it and do all we can to help you realize it. (See Intrinsic 16 in the table.) Motivators 9 through 16 are what really turn us on. As we tap into their power through opportunities for satisfaction, there is no limit to what we can attain together.

You have a little genius inside, waiting to express itself. Knowing your life purpose, and having a passion to fulfill it, brings out your genius. No one can be you and use your gift as well as you can.

Thank you for your contributions thus far. As we do a better job of meeting your needs, let your gifts shine for all to see. If there is something we can do better, we'd like to know. I, and the firm, wish you maximum success throughout your career with us, or wherever you believe best supports your purpose.

CEO's name and signature

20

NEEDS-EQUITY REALITY

Strength lies in differences, not in similarities.
— STEPHEN COVEY

A MAJOR SOCIAL BENEFIT OF SATISFYING Smart16 work needs is attaining equity among staff members and between staff and their managers. In my research during South Africa's apartheid era, the satisfaction of several intrinsic needs for all racial groups cut their turnover from 56 percent to 26 percent in one year. It was sustained thereafter. Retention of three quarters of staff in this one job position saved the firm bucketsful over the next 17 years. The next chapter chronicles that investigation and field test in work-need satisfaction.

As work-need gaps are closed for each group, feelings of exclusion or diminishment dissipate. Needs-equity overrides or diminishes overt and unconscious biases. Future Smart16 surveys indicate the degree of compliance with, or indifference to, a firm's social objectives. In the table below, effective strategies target needs-equity across the spectrum of work motivators:

Motivators: I Need (1–8); I Desire (9–16)	Needs-Equity Strategies
1. To be treated fairly and equally with others.	Issues may stem from overt or unconscious biases, causing inequitable treatment. Redirect staff by clarifying needs-equity. Gain proactive support for social policies and initiatives. Entrench leadership/nurturing competencies. Monitor, reinforce progress against the needs-equity standard.
2. To have my group's acceptance.	Overt or latent biases hamper inclusion. Emphasize policy over person: No one may be treated as if inferior in value. Guide close-knit groups to absorb new and minority members. Use team activities to display everyone's talents and contributions. Reward fairly and equitably.
3. To have the necessary tools, resources, information, and instructions to do my job.	Favoritism causes inequitable support and resource allocation. Who lacks something needed? Is it due to you? Provide equitably to all by closing individuals' need gaps.
4. To be trusted to do good work.	Granting trust to all will forge relationships. Assign tasks and responsibilities equitably. Include all in expressions of confidence.
5. To always know what my boss expects from me.	Communications are equally vital to all. Allocate time equitably to share expectations. Probe for concerns about meeting them. Guide and support as individuals require, regardless of their differences.
6. To have a supportive boss who helps solve problems that affect me.	Intervene when problems manifest. One-on-one, explore the nature and sources of the problem. Apply policy fairly to effect resolution. Seek help from HR and/or your manager if an issue persists. Assure each of his or her value to the firm. Maintain an open-door policy for grievances.

7. For my work unit/ department to be well-organized.	Organize work and resources equitably based on the best interests of individuals and firm. Respond to Smart16 gaps through group and one-on-one meetings to obtain everyone's input.
8. To receive good pay and benefits and fair evaluations of my performance.	Race, gender, sexual orientation, and ethnicity shall not create inequity in pay, benefits, or performance reviews. Strictly and vigilantly apply policy governing these sensitive areas.
9. To have work that interests and challenges me and that makes the best use of my skills.	Talents are distributed equitably in the population. Opportunities to apply them may not be. Tailor work assignments by gifts and skills. More gets done. Each must have equal opportunities to earn satisfaction.
10. To grow my competencies, knowledge, skills, and experience through my job.	Expanding individuals' capabilities will engage them. Grow them with challenging, tailor-made projects; train continually in more complex tasks. Delegate some of your work to each associate to grow them.
11. To have the autonomy and authority to perform my job as I think best.	Being one's own boss is motivating. It spawns 'intrapreneuring'. Task ownership inspires creativity and innovation. Natural abilities are amplified. Confidence is developed.
12. To know that my work is contributing to the organization's goals.	Staff develops self-worth by knowing the impact of their work. Explain how their work affects outcomes for colleagues and down the line. Reinforce individual value.
13. To receive recognition and rewards for my performance.	Opportunity, recognition, and reward must be equitably afforded. Performance varies by opportunity, skill, and guidance/ support. Create optimal conditions for all to earn rewards.
14. To relate well with my colleagues and have their respect.	Interpersonal biases inhibit social policy and objectives. All players on a team have equal obligations to meld the team through respect, support, and collaboration. Giving and receiving must be kept in balance. Apply policy.

JOSEPH COX

15. 15. To participate in decisions and have my suggestions valued.	Staff has valuable input about their jobs. Top-down initiatives need bottom-up buy-in. Equitably solicit all staff members' ideas and solutions. Collaborate to increase participation and agreement.
16. To have the opportunity to advance and achieve my life's purpose.	Aspirations for a better job and a fulfilled, purposeful life are universal work needs. Recruitments, promotions, and opportunities must statistically reflect the racial, ethnic, and gender composition of the population.

Needs-equity serves every gender, ethnicity, and sexual orientation. Needs-equity policy mandates it. Gaps due to biases or other factors are closed. When the workplace fosters mutual respect and harmony, people adapt to that norm. It is in their economic and social interest.

Each strategy is drilled in via DiaplanU. Offending behaviors erode as inclusive ones develop. Caring for our neighbors, as they are, fills the third bucket of profit. Going through that experience changes a manager's perspective on what he or she is doing and why.

Factoid: Tiny worker bees pollinate the plants that feed the world. They get all the honey they need to do their jobs. Imagine if they didn't.

Keep Smart16 honey flowing to every "bee" an equitable share. Each has a critical job to do.

The Employee Experience

A sustainable, differentiated relationship is only partly about benefits, policies, and programs. Rather, it extends the consideration of worker needs to the broader workforce experience. Everything from well-being, personal and professional growth, and meaningful work is on the table.

The relationship also can't be one-sided. For an employer to be able to address the entire workforce experience, it needs to have an ongoing conversation with workers about what is important to them and why it matters. The point is to engage workers in a dialogue that gives the employer insight into what truly drives them, and that gives workers a meaningful voice about these deeper values. (https://www2.deloitte.com/us/en/insights/focus/human-capital-trends/2021/the-evolving-employer-employee-relationship.html)

Love and Win-Win

Intrinsic motivation doesn't correlate with race, ethnicity, or gender. We're all the same. Managers can satisfy their intrinsic motivators better than their staffs, of any makeup, can. But we are closing that gap. Managers must spend time working with each staff member to be familiar with their issues and discuss ways to enrich their jobs. Allocating time for them means caring—love. There is no justification for withholding it.

Needs-equity policy incentivizes managers who have yet to show altruism. What job content, personal development, level of autonomy, recognition, or life goals will inspire individual associates? The right mix (chapter 6) will take time to ascertain. Win-win rules when all staff is as intrinsically satisfied as their manager; or at a minimum, is progressing steadily toward it.

21

METRICS FROM AFRICA

*A fundamental concern for others in our
individual and community lives would go
a long way in making the world the better
place we so passionately dreamt of.*

—NELSON MANDELA

CAN NEEDS-EQUITY BE ACHIEVED IN a country where inequality is government policy? Clearly not. But is progress toward equity possible? The chance to try came in the early 1980s while working for Beares Ltd., in Durban, where this story began.

Bruce Hopewell, human resources director and a member of the company's main board, came to the training department to discuss an issue with me. We were reeling from 56 percent staff turnover in the credit departments of our furniture stores. I was aware of the problem as we were constantly conducting classes in credit counseling and lending to assist customers in purchasing furniture on credit. With about two thousand credit specialists in this role nationally, it was a costly statistic. Various studies reported that replacing an entry-level staff member costs about two months' salary.

Bruce asked me if training could get the numbers down. I said I would give it some thought. The company employed 16 regional administrative managers with oversight of the credit offices. I invited them to the training department for a day to brainstorm turnover.

Background

Credit offices were run by the *head ladies*. They were responsible for their sections, with oversight from the people who would brainstorm with me. The profile of a head lady was mid-forties to mid-sixties, a former housewife with children, who had left the nest, so she came to work for us. None had any training in managing people, although we trained them in credit processing and collections. Because the work was precise and mistakes were costly, supervision was close and critical. We weren't losing head ladies, just their staff at over 1,100 people per year.

Assessing credit risk among indigenous people was daunting. Thankfully, Beares was as fair and considerate as borrowers could hope for. Still, defaults and collection work could be emotional and onerous.

In preparing for the all-day session, I did some research. One article discussed turnover at a national level in the United States. The writer cited the research of social anthropologist Robert Ardrey, who spent many years in South Africa. Ardrey looked at US turnover statistics from a psychological angle. From 1929, when the stock market crashed, to 1945, the end of WWII, staff turnover in the United States was close to zero. Following the stock market crash came the Great Depression, aggravated by the dust bowl calamity in the US heartland in the 1930s. Then, the world was at war from 1939 to 1945. Those who had jobs held on to them. Unemployment was up to 50 percent. As soon as the war ended, turnover started climbing sharply. Within a few years, it reached levels that are common in industry today. I found Ardrey's summation of that phenomenon intriguing:

"The hungry psyche had replaced the hungry belly."

People began looking for more from their jobs. He had nailed it, but it didn't dawn on me right then. It was early morning, and the meeting was about to begin. I wrote a note next to the 9 a.m. time slot in my day planner—"Hungry psyches, hungry bellies" —then forgot it. Throughout the day we explored hiring, training, on-the-job training, management and supervision, salary, benefits, and competitors. Nothing stood out. Our competitors had similar stats. Maybe we had to live with it.

Around 3 p.m. I glanced at my planner and saw Ardrey's quote. I recounted the US scenario to the group for discussion on possible psychological factors at play. Was it plausible that hungry psyches caused staff turnover here? The notion was curious enough to expand our discussion. The more we got into it, the more promising it seemed. (Note that the meeting's focus was shifting from extrinsic motivators to intrinsic.) We began reviewing what the experts had concluded about motivation. Here is a recap of the final two hours.

First up was Abraham Maslow. I summarized his conclusions: Motivation is about fulfilling a hierarchy of needs in sequence from the bottom up. Levels 1 through 3 are survival-related. Levels 4 and 5 are the desire to flourish. While this summary cites the two types of motivators in the guru's lists, back then we did not distinguish them. Nor did Maslow by the terms we use today:

5. Self-Actualizing: to fulfill lifelong aspirations. ⎫
4. Self-Esteem: to feel good about one's self. ⎬ Intrinsic Motivators

3. Belonging: to have acceptance and protection of a group. ⎫
2. Security: to be free of environmental and physical threats. ⎬ Extrinsic Motivators
1. Basic: to satisfy hunger, thirst and shelter needs. ⎭

I asked, "Do our people leave to meet psychological needs elsewhere?

One regional exec responded, "Well if they are not leaving because of hungry bellies, what's left has to be in the psyche?"

I asked, "Is our problem rooted in apartheid or ethnic conflict?" Head ladies were Caucasian. Credit staff were Indian, mixed-race, Zulu, or one of ten other indigenous tribes.

Caucasians could be Afrikaans (Dutch descent), English, or a mix of white-only European immigrants. White Rhodesians had streamed into South Africa from what is now Zimbabwe.

"Is it possible, in this mixed-race office, to get harmony and productivity and hang on to the people we hire?" I asked.

Another executive replied, "Apartheid is going to be a barrier, but there is no reason we can't be a lot more caring about their job satisfaction."

"Hang on to that thought," I encouraged. "Let's see what the other gurus have to say."

We continued with Douglas McGregor. He introduced X and Y management styles (autocratic versus democratic) and the basic beliefs that drive corporate management styles. How much were head ladies involving staff in decision-making (Y-style management)? Participants felt we had room to grow this intrinsic motivator.

Next was Frederick Herzberg. His *Two-Factor Theory* (hygiene factors and motivators) contrasted extrinsic and intrinsic motivators, though he didn't name them as such. Having positive hygiene factors (extrinsic) doesn't mean people are satisfied or happy. Satisfiers (intrinsic) concern the work itself. Is it meaningful and rewarding? And job enrichment: Is staff challenged with increasing responsibilities and opportunities for personal development? If pastures were greener elsewhere, did we need to water our grass? We agreed. It looked more and more like we were very deficient in intrinsic satisfiers.

I asked a series of questions:

- Where are our credit offices on the X-Y continuum? (more X)
- Are our people inherently lazy? Must we push them to produce? (mixed result)
- Are we saying by word and action that if the staff doesn't make bad credit decisions, they get to keep their jobs? (probably)
- Do we value them as having the potential for higher responsibility, Y thinking? (generally, no)

We noted the duality all gurus grappled with:

- Needs and desires in Maslow.
- Dissatisfiers and satisfiers in Herzberg.
- X and Y in McGregor.
- Ardrey's two—bellies and psyches

Were there more twos we should look at? It was around 4:30 p.m., and we had been going all day. We sensed a solution was near. HR had brought in the leadership program mentioned in chapter 1. We had trained most managers in this concept. No surprise, it contained another *duality*: People are either *able and willing* or *unable and unwilling*.

If the gurus were right, and they were all addressing motivation, surely there was a strategy for us. It seemed like a good time to vote.

How many think we are not paying enough? No hands.

How many think we are not recruiting the right people? Two hands.

How many think we have poor office working conditions? No hands.

How many think we have dissatisfiers in the credit offices? Three hands went up.

"What are the dissatisfiers?" I asked. Two answered that it was how they were being supervised. Another referred to Maslow's security and belonging levels. People didn't feel secure in their jobs; maybe their environment was threatening.

"How many think the jobs themselves are dead end?" A few hands went up. I followed up. "So, we aren't doing much about the job enrichment Herzberg prescribed?" They conceded that we weren't.

"How many think we have a lower-order problem described in Maslow's bottom three and Herzberg's dissatisfiers?" One hand went up. When I asked what it was, the reply came, "It's micromanagement and/or company policy."

"Are we overdoing the X? Most agreed that we were in those jobs.

"How many think that if we train the Head Ladies to team build, grow their people's competencies, and satisfy their higher-order needs like self-esteem and job enrichment, turnover will go down?" Sixteen hands!

In ninety minutes, we had moved from a hypothesis—

> Unsatisfied psychological needs may contribute to staff turnover—

to a working theory—

> Managers will reduce staff turnover if they develop staffs' competencies, increase their self-esteem, and enrich their jobs.

A social anthropologist opened the door. Behind it was a call to lead credit staff to a more flourishing place. Seventeen in the room. Seventeen in consensus. But it would be 17 years before I could put a minimal dollar figure on the impact. It was after 5 p.m. and the admin executives wanted to hit their favorite watering hole. They deserved it, courtesy of the training department.

The next day, I briefed my staff on our objective: Design a training intervention targeting the leadership skills of our head ladies. We rolled it out three months later, twenty-eight modules that would take two years to complete throughout the country. We called it TOP GUYS. It sounds like a sexist misnomer today, but it was an acronym for *Training Of People, Guiding, Understanding Your Staff.* Credit goes to department secretary, Sharon Korb, for the acronym. The women didn't have a problem with it. Anne Crane, my credit training officer and a former head lady, gave it thumbs-up.

The guiding and understanding parts were strong clues that the dual skills of leadership and nurturing related to the two types of motivators. But what was the financial impact?

I left South Africa in 1984, a year after introducing TOP GUYS. I wouldn't know the impact on staff retention until 1989, when Bruce visited me in Tampa. Of course, I asked how TOP GUYS was doing. Credit office turnover fell from 56 percent to 26 percent the first year and stayed in the mid-20 percentile to date. The decline meant 5,600 people did not need recruitment and training over those five years. The knowledge and experience of over 1,100 people who stayed aboard made for very effective and efficient credit offices. At a cost of two months' salary to replace one person earning $750 per month, the saving was $1,500. At 56 percent turnover and 2,000 credit specialists, the annual turnover in 1983 was 1,120 people. At $1,500 per person X 1,120 people, the annual saving was $1,680,000.

TOP GUYS was still running in 2000, when my successor, Keith Brown, spent a few days in my Tampa home and confirmed it. Assuming the number of employees remained constant (it grew) and turnover remained at a lower rate (it did), and salaries remained at the same level for 17 years (no, but we'll leave it for ease of calculation and a conservative number), the cost savings over seventeen years was $28,560,000. Adjusted for inflation, that number in 2023 is $49,123,200. Satisfying intrinsic desires is a phenomenal people strategy!

This experiment based on motivational theory in a real-world corporate laboratory, yielded the theorized outcome. We attacked turnover with more intense, more frequent leadership behaviors targeting intrinsic motivators. Turnover fell by 53.5 percent. The theory that 17 executives adopted in 1983 is documented fact, reconfirmed annually over 17 years.

Would the reader imagine that the intervention would outweigh apartheid's negatives in the "Beloved Country"?* Frontline staff were turning over. Personal and professional growth by Head Ladies grew staffs' self-esteem and raised hope for the future. It was institutionalized caring.

I've been asked, "Did it really take that long to find an answer to the man's [Alec Rogoff's] questions?" To which I answer, "Everyone else had the same amount of time I did, and they didn't answer the questions." As slow as I was, others were slower. They never met Mr. Rogoff.

I and Dr. Rodriguez conducted three more multiyear studies since 2005. Desired effects emerged in multiple countries and cultures. Causes had been identified and were controlled. The reliability of data and the conclusions drawn from it are replicable.

Additional studies hardened findings. We tested the impact of other variables. Positive correlations rose over time, but marginally. None of The Smart16 were dislodged by more potent independent variables. Below, tangible dollars ($$), box 6, emerge when all boxes before it add value; the first two boxes being the most crucial. They're the *big give* that brings the *big get* at the end.

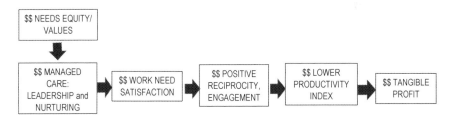

This John Dryden quote could refer to a dive into intangibles to avert productivity errors in the tangible realm:

---

* Nelson Mandela's dream about "concern for others" came true in a small corner of his *Beloved Country*, a reference to *Cry, the Beloved Country* (Alan Paton, 1948), a worldwide best-selling novel about interracial life in South Africa.

Errors like straws upon the surface flow. He who would search for pearls must dive below.

My Employee Experience

At another Denver firm, I was asked to deliver a truckload of goods urgently needed by a customer and was directed to a truck that I hadn't driven before. I left the loading bay and pulled into the street. When putting on the brakes at the first red light, the pedal went all the way to the floor. I was able to stop by gearing down and using the emergency brake. That's how I managed to deliver the load and return to the warehouse. Enroute back, a light turned yellow as I approached a major intersection. This time, gearing down and applying the emergency brake couldn't get it stopped. Cars zipped through on the cross street ahead of other drivers, who slammed on brakes and blared their horns as I ran the light.

Things happen during customer service if we don't take care of those providing it. What if the last person to drive that truck was a supervisor? Caring replaces errors with pearls.

22

SOFT-SKILLS PEDAGOGY

*Soft skills get little respect but they
will make or break your career.*

—PEGGY KLAUS

PART OF THIS RESEARCH WAS determining why vendors' management training didn't transfer to the job. Remember, this saga began with me complying with a mandate from the big boss of a billion-dollar company. Impediments in instructional design were preventing the written or spoken word from incarnating as work behavior. Until incarnation occurs, being an extra-mile manager is only an aspiration. The disciple, John, referenced this phenomenon when describing his teacher: "The Word became flesh and dwelt among us." So how do we incarnate the spoken and written word? Transference requires very deliberate, planned actions. What are the impediments to that?

Three myths are fatal to soft-skills learning transfer:

1. Learning and doing are two separate acts.
2. Large learning doses are cost-effective and economical.
3. The classroom is the best medium for management and soft-skills training.

Myth #1: Learning and Doing Are Two Separate Acts

"First you learn, then you do." This notion from John Holt's book, *Instead of Education (Sentient Publications, 2003)* shows the barrier to soft skills transfer from the classroom to the job. Holt helps us grasp that learning and doing are the same things. Application on the job is when, where and how behavioral learning occurs.

"Not many years ago I began to play the cello. I love the instrument, spend many hours a day playing it, work hard at it, and mean someday to play it well. Most people would say that what I am doing is 'learning to play the cello'. But these words carry into our minds the strange idea that there exist two very different processes: (1) learning to play the cello; and (2) playing the cello. They imply that I will do the first until I have completed it, at which point I will stop the first process and begin the second; in short, that I will go on learning to play until I have learned to play and that then I will begin to play."

"Of course, this is nonsense. There are not two processes but one. We learn to do something by doing it. There is no other way. When we first do something, we will probably not do it well. But if we keep doing it, have good models to follow, and helpful advice if and when we need it, and always do it as well as we can, we will do it better. In time, we may do it very well. The process never ends."

"Educators talk all the time about 'skills' … (But) as Whitehead said years ago, we cannot separate an act from the skills involved in the act. The baby does not learn to speak by learning the skills of speech and then using them to speak with, or to walk by learning the skill of walking and then using them to walk with. He learns to speak by speaking, to walk by walking. When he takes his first hesitant steps he is not practicing. He is not getting ready. He is not learning how to walk so that later he may walk somewhere. He is walking because he wants to walk right now."

Learning soft skills is the act of practicing them on the job, period. We have workshops, and we have work on the job. The twain has never met, so as to measurably increase engagement, productivity, and profit. Un-engagement (lack of motivation) and disengagement (negative reciprocity and spite) characterize two thirds of the workforce in most firms. To supplant myth #1 and satisfy work needs, soft skills must be practiced (learned) one at a time.

To visualize ourselves performing an act, we must focus on that act alone. Our minds don't focus on two things at once. We can't hear and comprehend two statements at the same time or speak two statements at once. Thoughts occur one at a time. Actions can only be executed one at a time. If you have ever tried to catch a ball and throw one simultaneously, one of those actions has your focus, while the other action is not successful. How are we ignoring this fact?

Classroom-based management training presents many process steps for a range of soft skills, plus role-playing for each. Familiarization and memorization are useful. But precisely how do written and verbally communicated processes incarnate as job behavior? By deliberate, planned actions, one at a time. Is it orchestrated that way in the current paradigm? There is little value without utility. How many of us digest and apply a seminar manual's content back on the job? But if we decide to intensely and frequently care, and act on it, incarnation of training is a feasible endeavor.

The classroom serves for group brainstorming, problem-solving, team-building, and other structured practices with colleagues. The general rule is: Allow learners to self-direct except where a classroom is needed. Let's tackle the dosage myth.

Myth #2: Large Learning Doses Are Economical

Trainers cover a lot of ground with as many participants as manageable. The Ebbinghaus Curve of Forgetting[*] refutes such economics. Several other researchers experimented with a learner's capacity to absorb and process information. In 1956, George A. Miller discussed the 'magical number' of concepts an individual can grasp at one time. In 1974, Herbert A. Simon investigated learning 'chunks' and endeavored to identify the maximum-sized chunk people can process in a learning-assimilation situation. John N. Warfield, in 1988, dealt with the magical number of concepts individuals can grasp with any utility. While Miller's and Simon's studies show this number to be very conservative, between five and seven, Warfield contended that the number is three, plus or minus zero.

Warfield introduced the *span of knowledge integration* (SKI) and showed that because of lattices that affect the analysis and synthesis of information, each new chunk of information added to a lattice has a negative geometrical impact on SKI due to multi-relational factors. While this simplifies his findings, the relevance for cognitive and behavioral development is noteworthy: It appears we can absorb three concepts at one time. Beyond that, integration rapidly declines.

In a workshop of four hours, dozens of concepts are disseminated. Few are recalled or used when SKI is exceeded. The likelihood of this after most workshops and seminars is 100 percent.

Validation of impact is, accordingly, elusive. The Ebbinghaus curve of forgetting then kicks in. Utility becomes an afterthought. Counting attendees trained shows trainers were hard at work. Regarding the fruit of that work, headcount overlooks the element of behavioral learning.

This illustration explains the dosage issue in training delivery:

---

[*] https://www.mindtools.com/a9wjrjw/ebbinghauss-forgetting-curve.

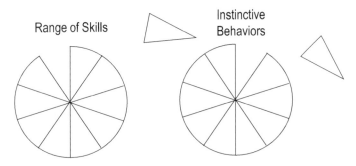

Range of Skills   Instinctive Behaviors

The diagram above shows a skill supplanting an instinctive behavior. A learner can only focus on changing one behavior at a given instant. Unless the desired behavior (skill) is singular, explicit and relevant to the situation at hand, there is little motivation to learn via practice. When the desired technique is subject to recall or has to be distilled from an ambiguous body of material, no practice (learning) will ensue.

Learning is always based on need or interest (motivation). In a work context, the need is the situation at hand and its implications for the learner. If the learner perceives that the application of the technique will satisfy their need for job performance, recognition, personal growth, increased responsibility and advancement, there is motivation to learn, i.e. attempt a technique on the task at hand. Training concepts involving behavioral modification (supplanting instincts or habits with proven skills) must fit learner's work context and be accessible on-demand. Few development programs apply these conditions. Fewer still can measure the impact on productivity and profit.

Source: Author's 2003 web article: *Adult Learning Principles*

An Analogy

When eleven men on an NFL team take the field with the ball against the opposing team, they huddle before each play. During the huddle, each player receives an assignment for the upcoming play. Each player has one, and only one thing to do—run a pass pattern, block, create a screen, throw or catch a pass and so on. No single player is expected to do more than one thing for that play. Still, mistakes are made. Unexpected situations develop from the defending team's reactions, so no guarantees of success exist, though plays are extensively rehearsed. Now imagine if that same team had only one huddle at the beginning of each possession. If all plays were called for the next series of downs and each player had to remember which action to take during each play, would skills be incarnated and executed?

Multiple plays can't be called in advance due to offensive play outcomes and the defending team's reactions. Similarly, plays called in a classroom can't anticipate reactions from those with whom those plays will be used. Getting derailed when using a behavioral model is common.

We now know that if the thing focused on is something being learned, it has to be a small chunk. Corporate learners exit classrooms with pages of notes and maybe visualizations of making plays on the job. Yet, application is inversely proportional to information volume. The longer the time frame between the play call and the execution, the less effective players will be. The long huddle is over and we are on our own, largely winging it.

Due to its shortcomings, the classroom role should be limited to the functions mentioned previously. Self-directed learning in small bites should follow any classroom soft-skills experience to integrate concepts and processes with real-time activities. Digital learning, in appropriately small doses, does the trick. Even this will fail to dislodge counterproductive behaviors if particular skills are not matched to specific situations and people requiring them. More on this next chapter.

First, let's synthesize the research of numerous clinical researchers on adult behavioral learning. Instructional design should be measured against these criteria. If not, forget about documenting positive impact from application:

1. Learning occurs in small doses.
2. Learning requires practice and reinforcement for full assimilation.
3. Learning new behaviors requires a change in beliefs or motivations.
4. Learning occurs best when the learner personally benefits.
5. Learning is best measured with the clinical processes of:

a. Self-Assessment, b. Cognitive Measures,
c. Behavioral Measures

Remember also that developing leadership and nurturing skills is about increasing their intensity and frequency. That takes assigned strategies, application attempts, measurement, feedback, and accountability.

Myth #3: The Classroom Is the Best Medium for Soft-Skills Training

The notion that management training by its nature should only be conducted in a classroom is flawed. It arose not because of proof that it's the best medium. It's simply easier to orchestrate—pick a topic, pick a group. Sessions concern information delivery more than utility. But who would bring a group together for three chunks? So, we give them many chunks.

The emergence of Performance Support Systems (PSS) is evidence that the classroom has not been enough. Good thinking, but the nomenclature is misleading. PSS connotes that learning has occurred and simply needs to be supported. *Job aids are the learning vehicles.* Cognitive aspects presented in the classroom are only an introduction. That can be communicated in a variety of ways without assembling a group.

A major barrier to on-the-job practice is the format of classroom learning materials. These consist of a binder covering the seminar or workshop. They may contain scores of pages, or a hundred or more, covering many competencies. Learners return to their offices or desks and store these binders on a shelf somewhere. While this is logical for space reasons, a subtle decision has been made—to put the materials out of immediate sight and use before the competencies are mastered.

It takes a high level of motivation to go to the shelf, obtain the binder, return to the desk, and then search through copious materials looking for content applicable to a variety of daily priorities. It is not a natural, easy process for the learner. Defaulting to instincts is the norm. I call this the "proximity problem." The farther the training is from the learner in time and space, the less likely the utility.

Then there is the absence of managerial support of classroom training. What materials are provided to supervisors of classroom participants for coaching, feedback, and reinforcement? The following graph demonstrates what happens to classroom training that is not reinforced:

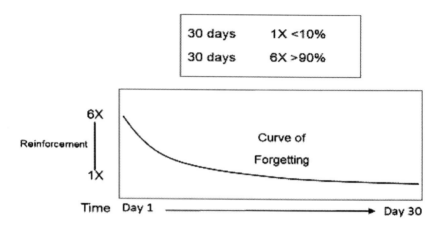

Source: Albert Mehrabian's research, referenced in his book *Silent Messages.*

If people are exposed to an idea one time, less than 10 percent is retained in thirty days. If they are exposed six times, with interval reinforcement, more than 90 percent is retained after thirty days. Are supervisors of classroom participants assigned responsibility to reinforce what is *learned?*

Learners are sent to workshops facilitated by trainers who can't reinforce on the job. The learner's supervisor is not likely to reinforce. The learner bypassed him or her on the way to the workshop and on the way back to the job. Bosses may not be familiar with the workshop content. Therefore, they may be unprepared to give feedback. A measurable rise in productivity and profit from soft skills is a fantasy until we orchestrate application.

Factoid: If we lie to ourselves and believe it, we are not only dishonest, we're also gullible.

A behavioral skill develops when it is matched to a task that calls for it using a deliberate, planned act. That has to be an easy step. As simple as deciding what situation on a to-do list offers a development opportunity. This is intentional learning. We must time-activate utility.

Chapter 11, "The Dirty Dozen," summarized causes that obstruct engagement. We cited the $166,000,000,000 spent by US firms annually on leadership training. Behavioral change impacting engagement has been barely noticeable since 2000. We showed why that training did not transfer to the job. A learning system based on scientific findings was a must to develop. It has to correlate highly with rising productivity, lower staff turnover, and higher profits. Focus on work needs makes it happen. ROI depends on that focus. The toolbox maintains that focus.

Chapter 23 juxtaposes learning content and work needs. The twain finally meets.

23

INCARNATING INSTRUCTION

Start by doing what is necessary, then what is possible, and suddenly you are doing the impossible.

—ST. FRANCIS OF ASSISI

As AN EXAMPLE OF 'DOING' let's imagine we're on a learning track in DiaplanU. We open a new module, "Mentoring," a *necessary* for building a fully competent team:

- Learning to mentor effectively is both a cognitive and a behavioral process.
- The mentoring concept is cognitive. Turning that concept into a skill is behavioral.
- Dose sizes must be small in both cognitive and behavioral learning.

Applying the wisdom of St. Francis:

1. The necessary thing is deciding to improve the productivity of a certain staff member.
2. The possible thing is grasping the concept dose (from DiaplanU) and applying it today.

To do so, we block out a ten-minute time slot in our calendar to bridge the concept and behavioral steps to the job (intentional learning). The small dose looks like this:

The Objectives:
To create and maintain a warm coaching atmosphere.
To improve your existing relationship and your credibility as their manager.
To help your team member discover the how's and why's that will increase their abilities, plus solve the immediate issue or problem.

The Introduction:
Welcome and encourage.

Clarify Areas of Concern:
Identify the gap between the team member's existing and desired capability. Invite the team member to clarify what he or she already knows, understands, and can do.

List Alternative Solutions:
It's the team member's job, so implementation is up to them. The team member must generate possible solutions or ideas.

Agreement on the Best Solution:
Even if our staff member approached us for advice, should we fix it? No. If we want longer-term development and problem-solving abilities, we ensure that they take ownership. We are coaching, not playing their positions on the team. So jointly analyze possible solutions for positive and negative effects. Continue this approach until there is agreement on the best solution.

3. The impossible: It's a bite of learning we wouldn't normally imbibe. We would have probably fired on instincts or not mentored at all, yielding a mediocre or worse outcome.

Print out the steps for the mentoring session, or dictate them into your smart phone. A handy, in-proximity track to run on obviates guesswork. You are orchestrating soft-skills transfer.

> *Factoid: Timely advice is like a golden apple served on a silver platter. King Solomon.*

Some readers might be wondering, *what if I need a just-in-time bite, but I don't know where it is in DiaplanU?*

By the time learners have finished the modules assigned, they will have transferred 200 bites to their jobs. Once a module has been completed, all its content is accessible on demand. Learners will be familiar with learning unit titles. These guide them to the unit(s) needed on the fly. There are 500 bites (learning units) of professional and soft skills in DiaplanU. To access them all, learners can complete every track. Professional development continues toward mastery.

Remember, we are growing both leadership and nurturing competencies. The mentoring example was about increasing the intensity and frequency of leadership competency. The staff member targeted was *led* to a better level of performance. Let's look at two more examples, one calling for nurturing competency and one for professional competency.

One of the managers in a research client's firm slowly becomes aware of a bottleneck. She investigates and finds that Kesha, a staff member, is overcome by her workload. Kesha's upset. The manager has completed the problem-solving module. She selects this process from a learning unit to help Kesha become more efficient. Then she schedules a one-hour session with her. Steps taken in seeking an agreed solution are in parentheses:

> *Define the Problem (What):* In defining the problem, the manager identified the gap between the current situation and the desired one. (The staff member should be on track but is not.)

Collect Information: She identified the issues associated with the problem, incidental and major. (The staff member can't complete tasks quickly enough to meet all goals. Tasks have piled up.)

Establish the Real Cause (Why): What is the problem, and why does the person have it? Without adequate information, one can't put the puzzle together. (There are two issues: [1] Staff members did not receive sufficient training on the complex software system used for tasks. [2] The colleague who had been helping her left on maternity leave four weeks ago.)

Generate Alternative Solutions (How): The chance of a quality solution increases with multiple alternatives. This is where creativity comes into play. (The manager and staff member explored and documented a range of alternatives.)

Evaluate Solutions and Decide (What, When, How): The manager and Kesha decide on the best solution from the alternatives generated. (Best alternatives: Vendor offers two additional days of training in the software system, scheduled for the following week. Kesha's goal is temporarily revised in light of impediments.)

Prevent Future Problems (What If): Take actions to minimize the negative effects of a decision. For example, when changing a procedure in one's work unit, wouldn't one communicate it to the people it affects? (All recruits will receive two additional days of training from the software vendor.)

Implement: Things can go wrong during implementation. Remain flexible and be open to adjustments. (After implementation, an experienced "buddy" was assigned to Kesha for the next few weeks as needed.)

Follow-Up: Continue to follow-up until the problem has disappeared. (Done. Issue resolved.)

Kesha didn't need leadership. Her issue concerned extrinsic need 6: "Have a supportive boss who helps solve problems that affect me." She needed support and nurturing. That behavior hadn't come in time or was weak or absent. Intentional learning increased nurturing's frequency and intensity. Productivity rose. Kesha was retained and is performing well. Next Smart16 Survey showed the gap on the related question had narrowed from *Often* to *Seldom*.

This situation also alerted the manager to always provide what is needed *when it is needed*. A four-week gap caused a bottleneck and productivity decline. Who needs guidance or support today? Right now? Every unsatisfied work need inhibits performance.

A quick professional skill bite kept a manager from making the same mistake that cost his firm a lot of money. In his last round of negotiations for cafeteria supplies, he made a big price concession, but got nothing in return. He had completed "Negotiations Skills 1" but had yet to master the skills of this complex task. He had forgotten to apply the guidelines on concessions. He wasn't going to blow it on another tit for no tat. In three minutes, he copied this bite from unit 8 of "Negotiating Skills 1":

> When Making Concessions:
>
> - Make many small ones rather than a few large ones.
> - Get a concession back for every one you give.
> - Trade concessions carefully. Give a small one to get a larger one back.
> - Don't rush to make concessions. Once offered, they are difficult to withdraw.

With a targeted bite (guideline) learners can prepare to apply a strategic professional skill. Dictating or typing these into a smartphone keeps them handy. It provides a hedge against red ink on part of the deal, or being caught off guard with nothing to reference or fall back on.

Juxtaposing any of the 500 bites is placing an asterisk (*) on a to-do item in Outlook (or other agenda) that needs the matching bite from DiaplanU. What was substantially impossible under the old paradigm becomes normal as enterprises orchestrate soft-skills transfer. Pragmatic learning, appropriately dosed, offers just-in-time access. It's learners' black-ink bank for its ATM-like access. Content targets the Smart16. Needs-equity, institutionalized (the possible), helps fund wealth creation globally (the impossible). Thanks, St. Francis!

The reader's next steps are: (1) Weigh up the binary choice in chapter 25, and (2) acquire the toolbox to institutionalize needs-equity in the reader's organization.

We've learned that 68 percent of US managers are stuck on the first mile because people aren't given what they need in a timely, thorough manner. Enlightened managers give it through leadership and nurturing. The secret sauce is caring. Those who don't care will bear apathy's liability. The simple Smart16 Survey identifies the empathetic and apathetic. The PI of the latter puts a red dollar number on their tabs.

Let's close this chapter with Luke 6:38. It encapsulates cause-effect from giving and positive reciprocity. Where else can you find a guaranteed outcome on altruistic soft skills? The motivator that drives giving, triggers others' motivators to give back.

> *Factoid: Give, and you will receive. A large quantity, pressed together, shaken down, and running over will be put into your pocket. The same measures you use for giving to others will be applied back to you.*

24

FORECASTING INTANGIBLES' ROI

*Invention is the most important product of man's
creative brain. The ultimate purpose is the complete
mastery of mind over the material world, the
harnessing of human nature to human needs.*

—NIKOLA TESLA

IN ADVANCING OUR QUEST TO harness human nature to serve
human needs, milestones help us keep our bearings and motivation.
Milestones are more predictable when proven inputs are in place.
The number one input of mind over material for our subject here is
intrinsically motivated staff. That depends on their managers. Yes, the
acquisition of extrinsic satisfiers keeps people in the game, but it won't
make them shine like stars. That's about inspiration and a system
managers use to trigger and sustain it. Acquisition + Inspiration =
New Bottom Line.

If readers implemented this system in their firms, what results would
appear and when? The chronology below covers three years— the time
needed to institutionalize needs-equity. Each survey and associated
corporate report—after the benchmark inaugural study—will show
rising work-need satisfaction. After the third survey, the first evidence

of a declining PI appears. It yields a precise dollar figure on increased profit, evidence of positive financial impact (chapter 9). Departments' anomalies, highlighted in each Smart16 corporate report, are investigated for causes and solutions.

Smart16 Milestones:	Forecast of results from institutionalized work-need satisfaction over three years (nine Smart16 surveys). Monitor actual results against forecast.
Survey #1 Year 1	The benchmark Productivity Index (Payroll ÷ Revenues = PI) is calculated for corporate and all departments before the launch of the system. All future survey results are compared to the benchmark's metrics. Turnover statistics and trends are also captured. Rising need satisfaction and declining PIs are correlated (by licensed vendor) after each Smart16 survey.
	The first survey shows that departments with high need satisfaction have lower PIs. Where these two do not positively correlate, they are anomalies to investigate.
Survey #2	The second survey reinforces correlations between work-need satisfaction and lower PIs. Favorable trend lines on work-need satisfaction begin exhibiting. Investigate peak and valley anomalies department by department, manager by manager. Managers with higher need satisfaction will trend toward lower staff turnover. Institutionalizing needs-equity gradually reduces anomalies.
Survey #3	By the third survey (eight months after the first), definite trend lines have formed. PIs will be inversely proportional to need satisfaction trend lines. Finance can begin calculating payroll savings by comparing the benchmark PI with latest PIs. Each one percent decline in the PI has added one percent to profit.
Smart16 Year 2	**Milestones:** Forecasted results are being borne out by metrics derived from Smart16 surveys and analytics derived from Smart16 corporate reports.

Survey #4	By the fourth survey (beginning of year 2), trends are more pronounced. Peaks and valleys in need satisfaction have moderated as institutionalizing expresses its effect. By the fourth survey, four analytics should all be favorable: - Strong rising trend on corporate work-need satisfaction. Bell curves shifting right. - Many managers' work-need satisfaction levels reach 20/25 (extra-mile caring). - Falling corporate and department PIs (with savings) accrue extra profit. - Falling turnover with attendant cost savings in recruitment and training. Anomalies are investigated. Take corrective action to obviate them.
Surveys **#5 and #6**	By the end of year 2, there is a marked decline in staff turnover and substantially lower PIs. Savings, as calculated against benchmark PIs, will be substantial (2 to 3 percent of revenues). Profits will have risen proportionally.
Smart16 Years #3 and beyond **Surveys #7 to #9**	By the end of year 3, the needs-equity system will be well institutionalized. All metrics will be favorable: Smart16 scores, PIs, turnover decline, and higher profits (4 to 6 percent of revenues or higher). The corporate mission is being fulfilled more thoroughly and in less time. Social objectives (improved organizational climate, needs-equity metrics) benefit from better funding and better executive and downline support. Consider monetary rewards to staff and to units and departments that achieved higher profits from declining PIs.
Surveys #10 onward	Year 4 and onwards: Continue with surveys and online behavior/skill development. Without these, institutionalization corrodes, behavior degrades. Recidivism is detrimental to staff's interests and to the firm's financial and social interests.

Actions for Optimum Results

C-Suite Tasks:

1. Needs-equity is set as corporate policy.
2. Ensure institutionalizing of the system is driven and sustained by chains of command.
3. The finance department sends managers their PI metrics following each Smart16 Survey. Managers display these prominently in their departments.
4. Each department head accesses Smart16 Survey results to begin preparing to give feedback.
5. Year 4 and onward: Continue thrice annual Smart16 surveys and online behavioral development. Maintain needs-equity policy. Apply reward system.

Chains of Command Tasks

1. Apply the system as intended and advised in *The Extra-Mile Manager.*
2. All managers read *The Extra-Mile Manager* and complete the two-day *The Third Bucket of Profit* workshop.
3. Set a high bar for managers in maximizing their teams' intrinsic motivators.
4. Include needs-equity metrics as a fixed item on managers' meeting agendas.
5. Resolve statistical anomalies in corporate reports that obstruct institutionalizing of needs-equity.
6. These executive actions augment needs-equity and the financial gains accrued from high productivity. Audit each to optimize results.
7. Decide on a course of action for managers who remain apathetic toward work needs.

Human Resources Tasks

1. Revise managers' job descriptions to include accountability for work-need satisfaction.
2. Modify managers' performance bonuses so that 25 percent of the annual score, plus declining PI from managers' departments, reflect work-need satisfaction, with a minimum 20/25 score to qualify for a bonus.
3. In conjunction with chains of command, enroll managers and staff in online learning provided with the system.
4. Publicly recognize managers who score 20/25 or higher on Smart16 and/or whose departments' PI has declined.
5. Inculcate needs-equity responsibility in new managers at hiring and onboarding. Enroll new managers in *The Third Bucket of Profit* workshop after three months on the job.
6. Monitor the first year's Smart16 Survey results. Provide coaching or remedial training in the system to line/staff organizations (and its managers) as needed.

Factoid: When pressed to change our behavior, excuses pop into our heads.

Changing organizational behavior means changing the collective minds of our people. As we attempt it, the *Sisyphus Effect* kicks in. Sisyphus was king of Ephyra (present-day Corinth in Greece). Hades punished him for his maltreatment of people by forcing him to roll an immense boulder up a hill, only for it to roll back down every time it neared the top, repeating this action for eternity. Interestingly, St. Paul spent much time in Corinth and wrote two lengthy letters to his followers there. Perhaps he was familiar with the Sisyphus story. He wrote this familiar quotation to them: "Of all the works that I do, If I have not love, it profits me nothing." Joseph Conrad's novel *Victory* is predicated on the same theme.

Concerning business *profit*, every year we outlay big sums for leadership and management training. But we are pushing the boulder uphill if maltreatment—apathetic managerial behavior is tolerated. The interminable payback—negative reciprocity, un-engagement, disengagement and financial loss, keeps rolling back on us. But that boulder gets lighter as we institutionalize needs-equity. We get to the *Tipping Point* (below) quicker. By the end of year three, we have changed the collective mind. The *Snowball Effect* is positive reciprocity powered by intrinsic motivation. Behavioral futility transforms into momentum when caring ingratiates staff.

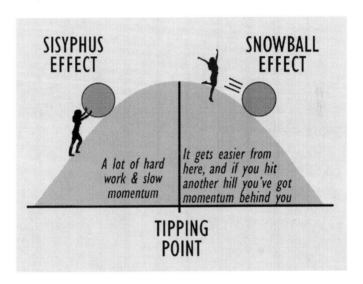

The Seatbelt Tipping Point

It took three decades for US drivers to end their resistance to mandatory seat belts. But two hundred million US drivers did it. Today it is nationally institutionalized. Our own and our passengers' well-being finally outweighed resistance. We learned to care about everyone's best interests, especially the millions of lives being saved. Liability insurance rates went down. There never was a good argument against seat belts.

Elizabeth Dole, US Secretary of Transportation, gave an ultimatum to US car makers: Install seatbelts in all vehicles by a specific date, or we will make you install the driver and passenger-side airbags. They didn't comply, so airbags became standard, as did seat belts. Her creative brain was at work. She led the nation and 200M drivers to do what was in everyone's best interest. Our nation passed the tipping point.

Institutionalization of needs-equity is in everyone's best interest. The well-being of people in our care will outweigh resistance to needs-equity. We'll learn to *give it*, just like we learned to *click it*. Institutionalization happens when leaders, like former secretary Dole, are creatively unrelenting. There is no good argument against needs-equity. Champions like Elizabeth Dole make it happen in their domains.

25

NEUROPLASTICITY DELIVERS

*Everything having to do with human training and
education has to be re-examined in
light of neuroplasticity.*

—NORMAN DOIDGE

THE ADAGE THAT THE LEOPARD doesn't change its spots generally
means people don't or can't change their thinking or behaviors. Over
the last forty years, and very profoundly in the last twenty, research has
shown that the brain's plasticity enables us to change how we think
and act.

Early researchers believed that neurogenesis, or the creation of new
neurons, stopped shortly after birth. Today, it's understood that the
brain's neuroplasticity allows it to reorganize pathways, create new
connections, and in some cases even create new neurons. Neurons that
are used frequently develop stronger connections. Those that are rarely
or never used eventually die. By developing new connections and doing
away with weak ones, the brain can adapt to the changing environment.[*]

Introducing needs-equity into human capital strategy changes the
corporate environment. The thinking and behaviors of managers toward

---

[*] https://www.verywellmind.com/what-is-brain-plasticity.

staffs that never faced scrutiny are now captured and reported. Hard numbers on how managers' behaviors impact productivity and profit are openly reviewed at every management level. Behavioral change strategies include policy, standards, behavioral modification and accountability. KPIs look very differently. The good news is that as difficult as behavioral modification is, our brains begin adapting when change becomes necessary for survival or advancement.

> Among other things, neuroplasticity means that emotions such as happiness and compassion can be cultivated in much the same way that a person can learn through repetition to play golf and basketball or master a musical instrument, and that such practice changes the activity and physical aspects of specific brain areas. (Andrew Weill, MD)

> Because of the power of neuroplasticity, you can, in fact, reframe your world and rewire your brain so that you are more objective. You have the power to see things as they are so that you can respond thoughtfully, deliberately, and effectively to everything you experience. (Elizabeth Thornton, educator and author)

> Our minds have the incredible capacity to both alter the strength of connections among neurons, essentially rewiring them, and create entirely new pathways. It makes a computer, which cannot create new hardware when its system crashes, seem fixed and helpless. (Susannah Cahalan, author of *Brain on Fire*)

Well-worn neural pathways that sustain poor habits, negative emotions, biases, and self-serving behavior can be replaced with new pathways that transmit and sustain prosocial behavior. The old neural pathways un-engage and disengage staff. The transformed work environment stimulates motivation and creativity. What was called idealism is now scientific strategy. It is our fiduciary duty to protect and grow our firms' human capital assets. Neuroplasticity supports our efforts.

A binary choice faces readers and their firms:

1. Continue to love yourself while overlooking some of your staff's work needs. Live with two-thirds of your workforce unengaged. Leave your brain wired with the current inequity paradigm. Forfeit profit from the third bucket. Forget about being a best place to work.

2. Love your neighbor as yourself, i.e., if you like it when your work needs are satisfied, then satisfy your staff's work needs. That's fair play. Renewed minds sustain needs-equity. Accrue third-bucket profit for the firm, its staff, and shareholders. Be a best place to work.

The choice is between mediocrity and excellence. Option 2 rocks because it sends all forms of win-lose inequities out the door, but our people stay and do so happily. What is in our third buckets and on our firms' annual reports will reflect management decisions concerning their people's well-being.

There is no third option. We have no reason to tolerate *The Great Gap* another day. Red-ink spigots in our brains will close as new neural pathways emerge. We are aligning motivational thought patterns with business goals.

For readers who want the mathematical version of this alignment, let's do a walk-through.

The output that we want is productivity. We discussed this earlier; we called it P. The statistical term for that output is the *dependent variable* (DV). Measures associated with productivity *depend* on input. The statistic for an input that may measurably affect the DV is the *independent variable* (IV).

In our case, the IV that changes the DV has two macro skills—leadership and nurturing. But there is more to this IV: The intensity and frequency (of macro skills' use) factor in. High intensity and high frequency use leave no sigma variances from the norm (the ideal output we seek). Variances correlate with lower productivity— not the DV we want. Here's the …

```
Diaplan Productivity Algorithm
     Hi L + Hi N = Hi P

        IV        DV
```

In plain English, if I always lead and nurture to meet my staff's work needs, they will be very productive. Or, when I go the extra mile for my people, I am simply doing what works best.

In 2016, we began a three-year study with an eight-hundred-employee finance firm in Central America. The firm was in the red when the CEO flew to Miami to meet with us. He was fairly new to this job. Staff turnover in his firm was around 40 percent, and climate surveys were unsatisfactory.

He decided to be a laboratory for our studies and introduced needs-equity. We trained every manager in the company to raise Smart16 Survey scores. All managers were also enrolled in DiaplanU and were completing required behavioral learning tracks.

Before the first year expired, the firm was in the black. Turnover declined several percentage points. By the end of the third year, the firm had grown to 1,200 employees. Staff turnover percentage dropped to the lower twenties. The firm continued to be profitable and attained a best place to work status. The PI dropped from 33 percent to 24 percent.

Neuroplasticity clearly played a role. Thinking patterns that caused 40 percent staff turnover made way for behaviors that satisfied staffs' work needs. Financial outcomes improved dramatically.

In December 2018, we began a three-year study with a four-hundred-employee financial services firm in Mexico. The last Smart16 Survey was conducted in July 2021. The firm was seriously in the red at inception. Well before the end of year three, it was generating record profits. The work-need satisfaction bell curve shifted strongly to the right, from a dotted line to a solid line (see below). Average need satisfaction scores on the Smart16 survey rose above 19/25, just short of the 80 percent (extra-mile) level, but close enough to overhaul management's and staff's behaviors.

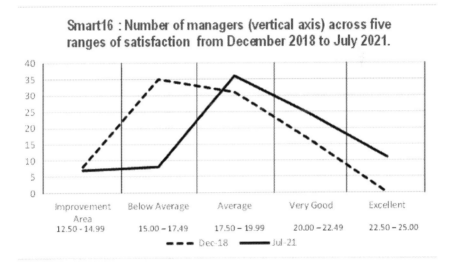

Smart16 : Number of managers (vertical axis) across five ranges of satisfaction from December 2018 to July 2021.

The staff of ninety managers (over 300 people) reported on their work-need satisfaction level. Manager scores were divided into five ranges, from "Improvement area" to "Excellent." The shift to the right shows that managers changed their behaviors to better satisfy staff work needs. The firm was institutionalizing needs-equity. The following table has the data used to construct the graph.

Smart16 Data: December 2018 vs July 2021

Smart16	Dec-2018	July-2021
Improvement Area	8	7
Below Average	35	8
Average	31	36
Very Good	16	24
Excellent	0	11
	90	86

Annual turnover rate, 2018: 55.9 percent. Annual turnover rate, 2021: 28.6 percent (down by half).

PI, December 2018: 37.9 percent. PI, July 2021: 33.7 percent (down 4.2 percent of revenues). Salaries were raised across the board during the course of the Study.

As new behaviors exhibit more frequently and more intensely, the brain is likewise changing. Improved behaviors become habitual, then second nature. Regression can occur if motivations degrade. Institutionalized needs-equity is a strong hedge against motivational decline, but it must be sustained. Continuance with the Smart16 Survey and DiaplanU, with ongoing accountability, maintains the improvements exhibited on year-end financials.

The firm grew by more than a hundred staff yet performed better with four fewer managers than in 2018. Revenues and profits reached the highest peaks in the firm's history by 2021.

In our final chapter, we'll see whether the IV, paycheck, correlates highly with the DV, empathy for staff needs.

26

HIRED-HAND SYNDROME: OFF RAMP

*The hired hand is not the shepherd, and
the sheep are not his own. When he sees the
wolf coming, he abandons the sheep and runs
away. Then the wolf pounces on them and scatters
the flock. The man runs away because he is a
hired servant and is unconcerned for the sheep.*

— PARABLE OF JESUS

THE PARABLE IS NOT ABOUT sheep, though applicable. It is about uncaring, salaried overseers. There is no correlation between salary and empathy.

> *Factoid: Failure to own our staffs' well-being causes insecurity, fragmentation and scattering.*

Let's bring this research to finality. When we see apathy, we scorn it; then hope outcomes waft innocuously into some void. But we do little else. We care about the employee experience but haven't yet made it company policy to care for their work needs. If not caring, what strategy serves staff aspirations? The employee experience craved is to have a job that turns them on and a boss who grows them. Short of those, nothing unfetters their potent work motivators.

Ownership of needs-equity is a chain of custody. Weak links—apathetic managers—decline ownership. When management connects apathy to losing half of corporate profit, needs-equity policy and practice will reach the tipping-point, then snowball. If we don't like the current *effect,* changing the *cause* is rational. Irrational apathy perpetuates the Sisyphus Effect.

Staff performances reflect our performance as managers. We're all at points on the apathy-empathy continuum (page 158). Our point on it predicts our performances as managers. Points fluctuate due to relationships, personal interests, and current business priorities. Empathetic managers don't only want their staffs to survive, they want them to flourish. Our migration to the right migrates our staff toward flourishing.

If our targeting isn't pragmatic, it is not felt and won't be reciprocated. Sincerity is paramount. How easy is it for any manager to slip into The Great Gap on just the first two of the Smart16? Consider an everyday example:

What People Want:

1. To be treated fairly and equally with others.
2. To have my group's acceptance.

What Is:

1. There is a small office clique that excludes others.
2. Sally and Maria gossip about Felipe and Louise.
3. The manager gives Randy the plumb tasks; Dante gets the onerous ones.
4. The manager's favorites get the window seats.
5. Gene's laptop is ancient and slow. Everyone else's is newer, faster.

6. Ana Lucia was hired two years ago. Brenda, hired this year, gets paid more for the same job.
7. Alec, a friend of the manager's son, gets to miss deadlines. Others get reprimands.
8. Sheila is often in the manager's office. The manager sees all others at their desks.
9. In staff meetings, the manager always calls on the same people for their opinions.
10. The manager gave three exemplary staff worse annual reviews than two mediocre favorites.

The hired-hand syndrome is operating. The want-is gap is glaring. The manager may be aware of some issues. Others arose imperceptibly. The beast that preys on this team is negligence. The team's attention is fragmented and resignations loom. The manager is neglecting or avoiding responsibilities, yet still gets a paycheck and a bonus. The C-suite is unaware of this gap. The firm is paying two salaries for one manager—the regular one and the extra cost for neglect.

Being directly responsible or allowing all ten demotivators to develop and fester is a common dysfunction. Smart16 scores are two to three sigma gaps from the norm (and there are fourteen other work needs). How bad can it get? By now we know. Being unaware and unresponsive are apathy traits. We chase off the wolf with intentional, pragmatic empathy. What does a turnaround look like?

One-on-one and group discussions to surface feelings are therapeutic. Admitting mistakes and pledging to improve, with accountability, shore up managers' integrity, credibility, and ownership. It's being micro-empathetic, precisely targeting each work need until all are satisfied. Overlooked gaps stay in the spotlight until closed.

On the continuum, we can reflect on the two to three sigma gaps that put us in the red zone (shaded gray area on the continuum's left; the lighter the shade, the more red ink) on certain survey responses. To migrate to the black zone by the next survey, we draw out staff feelings about deficient guidance and/or support from our end. We recommit to satisfying work needs and then give free rein to our primal prosocial instincts. Practice stimulates neurological changes that underpin macro skills. We inch toward the black zone.

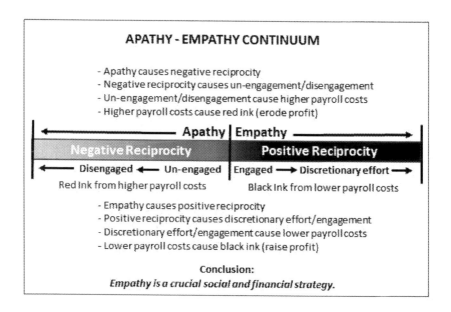

We grossly underestimated managers' roles when entrusting lives to their care. We didn't connect love for their people with their and their people's performances. That disconnect degraded care. It's our tragic, paradigmatic financial flaw. The management role is more shepherding, which requires personal care, than overseeing, which doesn't. Oversight doesn't align our people with our objectives.

Managing is derived from the Latin *manus*, for *hand*. For example, how trainers in Caesar's stables *handled* prized animals in their care. They were horse whisperers, who could turn unbroken horses into children's mounts. Similarly, managing people takes hands-on avid care and development.

Here's a real-life story on what prosocial behavior can do for every worker:

> Early in my career at Neiman Marcus (pre-laptops and cell phones), I had a boss who just got me: Jeremiah Murphy. He always trusted me to get the job done,

while simultaneously pushing me to go beyond the job description. In fact, he made sure I played *outside* my lanes and constantly encouraged me to adopt an entrepreneurial mindset - a now cherished skill of mine.

From finance to logistics, taught to negotiate for more— from others and from myself. Jerry Murphy represented disruption, innovation, and out-of-the-box thinking. He brought fun to every day and balanced it with a unique drive. He appreciated hard work, persistence, and ideas that would push the boundaries of how customers could experience the brand. Most of all, Jerry believed in the power of gratitude.

I remember going into his office one December morning after working 15 hours straight for 3 days in a row. We were going over the 4th quarter sales plan and I fainted. Totally passed out in his office. Jerry found someone to drive me home and, a few hours later, had soup from the Mermaid bar delivered. (This was way before Uber Eats or food delivery service!)

I will never forget this one act of kindness. It taught me that *a great boss goes the extra_mile* to show gratitude. The notion that gratitude matters is something I still believe. I surround myself *with leaders who care deeply* about each other and who challenge the status quo in pursuit of a common goal: to *nurture one's dream* and *grow gratitude* one garden at a time. (Donna Letier; emphasis mine. https://blog.gardenuity. com/6-stories-of-the-best-bosses/)

Do you recall Managing Director Rogoff's question?

"What is it they want from us that we're not giving them?"

Let's hear it straight from their mouths: "Treating us like we want to be treated—empathetically, lovingly, going the extra mile to meet our work needs."

That's it, Mr. Rogoff! We didn't ask them on your behalf. Our humblest apologies. Long overdue!

SUMMARY

Our mandate is to organize the nonobvious intangibles that correlate highly with ROI. Leadership and nurturing are the drivers. We will give bang for the buck, generate ROI, and eliminate buyer's remorse. Only intransigence, indifference or cowardice can deter us.

Globally, laborers yearn for intervention on their behalf. Maltreatment costs organizations $7 trillion worldwide annually (McKenzie & Company Report, August 2022). Needs-equity policy is our Nation's and the world's best hope for sustainable, inclusive growth. Unleashing human potential translates into high GDP. The decades ahead need massive wealth creation to raise everyone's living standards.

Transformations often fail, but we have all we need going for us. Every manager and associate become agents of transformation. We covered every strategy that contributes to the fruition of this transformation. Empathy and altruism are in our DNA to give and receive. Our chimp cousins set the example for us. Clan cohesion is also Homo sapiens' norm. Apathy is antisocial, yet pervasive under permissive management. As we focus on needs-equity, our minds are renewed. Red-ink neural pathways shrivel and die. The transformation that begins in the brain ends on the balance sheet.

The Extra Mile Manager is our operations manual for this humanitarian and financial imperative. As we say yes to that quest, we change at our core. Our mission strategy changes.

Our stickability and brainwork brought us to this launchpad. As we slough off apathy and embrace affection, we bring hope to those simply *surviving*. We make them *flourish*. The payback is our legacy.

Joe and Regina

AFTERWORD

For more information about institutionalizing needs-equity through the Smart16 Survey and DiaplanU, please call (954) 612-2140, or send an email to mail@diaplanonline.com with your contact information. You will be referred to a licensed consulting firm. Thank you for your readership and your continued interest.

BIBLIOGRAPHY

Cox, Joe, Zelaya, Julio. 2007. *What I Didn't Learn in My MBA, The Third Dimension of Profit.* The Learning Group Press.

Joe Cox, 2013, *Nail it Today, with Both Hands.* AuthorHouse.

Andrew Weil, M.D., 2011. *Spontaneous Happiness.* Little, Brown Spark.

Norman Doidge, M.D., 2007. *The Brain That Changes Itself: Stories of Personal Triumph from the Frontiers of Brain Science.* James H. Silberman Books.

Susannah Cahalan, 2012, *Brain on Fire*, Simon & Schuster.

Bassi, Lauri. 2004. *The impact of U.S. firms' Investments in Human Capital and Stock Prices.* (Research paper)

Klein, H. J. 1989. *An Integrated Control Theory Model of Work Motivation.* Academy of Management Review, 14: 150-172.

Leonard, N. H., Beauvais, L. L., & Scholl, R. W. 1995. *A Self Concept Based Model of Work Motivation.* Paper presented at the Annual Meeting of the Academy of Management, Vancouver, BC.

Richard Ryan/Edward Deci, 2016 Self-Determination Theory, Basic Psychological Needs in Motivation, Development and Wellness. Guilford Press

Porter, L. W., & Lawler, E. E. 1968. *Managerial Attitudes and Performance.* Homewood, IL: Richard D. Irwin, Inc.

Dawkins, Richard. 1990. *The Selfish Gene 30ᵗʰ Anniversary Edition,* Oxford University Press.

Diamond, Jared. 2006. *The Third Chimpanzee: The Evolution and Future of the Human Animal.* Harper and Company.

Halloran, Andrew. 2012. *The Song of the Ape.* St. Martin's Press.

Caudron, Shari. 2001, Nov. 4. *The Myth of Job Happiness, Workforce HR Trends $ Tools for Business Results.*

Graizer, Peter. 2001. *How to keep the team motivated over the long haul.* Recklies Management Project.

Sullivan, Jim and Kocenivich, Dick (August 2000) *Recognize the Importance of Incentives and Rewarding Employees.* Nation's Restaurant News.

Swift, Billie. (Sept 2001) *"Thank You" Goes A Long Way."* Risk Management. Risk Management Society Publishing, Inc.

Abraham Maslow. 1987. *Motivation and Personality,* Third Edition (Harper & Row).

F. Herzberg, B. Mausner, B.B. 1993 *The Motivation to Work.* Snyderman. Somerset, NJ: Transaction Publishers.

D. McGregor, 1960. *The Human Side of Enterprise.* McGraw Hill.

Kouzes, James M., Posner Barry Z. 2008. *The Leadership Challenge,* 4ᵗʰ Edition. Wiley and Sons.

John Holt. 2003. *Instead of Education, Ways to Help People Do Things Better.* Sentient Publications, LLC.

Bandura, A. 1986. *Social Foundations of Thought and Action: A Social Cognitive Theory.* Englewood Cliffs, NJ: Prentice Hall.

J.M. Syptak. *Altruism in Practice Management: Caring for Your Staff.* October 1998. Family Practice Management. 58-60.

B.B. Longest, P.E. Spector. 1997. *Job Satisfaction: Application, Assessment, Causes and Consequences.* Thousand Oaks, Calif: SAGE Publications.

P. Hersey, K.H. Blanchard, D.E. Johnson. 1996. *Management of Organizational Behavior: Utilizing Human Resources,* 7th Ed. Prentice-Hall.

LaRue, Michael D. 2002. *This Place is a Zoo, How to Manage the Unmanageable Organization.* iUniverse.

Howard, Pierce J., Howard, Jane Mitchell. 2001, *The Owner's Manual for Personality at Work.* Bard Press.

De Bono. Edward 1985, 1999. *Six Thinking Hats.* Back Bay books. Little, Brown and Company.

Lencioni, Patrick 2002. *The Five Dysfunctions of a Team: A Leadership Fable.* Josey Bass.

Blanchard, K., Zigarmi, P., Zigarmi, D. 1985. *Leadership and the One Minute Manager.* HarperCollins Publishers.

Covey, Stephen R. 2004. *The Seven Habits of Highly Effective People.* Free Press.

Klaas, Brian, 2021. *Corruptible: Who Gets Power and How it Changes Us.* Scribner.

Michael Graetz, 2004. *The Role of Architectural Design in Promoting the Social Objectives of Zoos. Part 2 Physical elements of Zoo Design.* Doctoral Dissertation.

Brassey, Jacqueline, de Smet, Aaron, Krayt, Michiel, 2023. *Deliberate Calm: How to Learn and Lead in a Volatile World*. McKinsey and Company

WEB REFERENCES

http://www.emory.edu/LIVING_LINKS/LL_2009/inequitypress1. html Quoting Jeanna Bryner, *Live Science* Staff Writer, Nov. 12, 2007.

http://www.livescience.com/15451-chimps-humanlike-altruism.html

http://www.livescience.com/4515-selfless-chimps-shed-light-evolution-altruism.html

http://www.brainhealthandpuzzles.com/brain_effects_of_altruism. html

http://www.huffingtonpost.com/2012/07/19/altriusm-brain-temporoparietal-junction_n_1679766.html

http://www.psmag.com/culture-society/scientists-locate-brains-altruism-center-43356/

http://www.childwelfare.gov/pubs/usermanuals/fatherhood/chaptertwo.cfm

http;//www.highered.mcgraw-hill.com/sites/dl/free/0073511722/ ... / Chap010.doc

http://www.cbr.cam.ac.uk/pdf/RR454.pdf

http://www.teambuildinginc.com/article_teammotivation.htm

http://www.rochester.edu/pr/Review/V72N6/0401_feature1.html

http://www.mba-courses.com

http://en.wikipedia.org/wiki/Servant_leadership

https://www.mindtools.com/a9wjrjw/ebbinghauss-forgetting-curve

Printed in the United States
by Baker & Taylor Publisher Services